Compact Guide: Milan is the ultimate quick-reference guide to this fascinating destination. It tells you all you need to know about Milan's attractions, from its majestic cathedral to its imposing Castello Sforzesco and from La Scala opera house to Da Vinci's *Last Supper*.

This is one of 133 Compact Guides, combining the interests and enthusiasms of two of the world's best-known information providers: Insight Guides, whose innovative titles have set the standard for visual travel guides since 1970, and Discovery Channel, the world's premier source of nonfiction television programming.

APA PUBLICATIONS
Part of the Langenscheidt Publishing Group

Insight Compact Guide: Milan

Written by: Gerhard Sailer
English version by: David Ingram
Updated and designed by: Clare Peel
Photography by: Jerry Dennis
Additional photography by: The Bridgeman Art Library 30/2;
Metropolitan Opera Archives 108; Ros Miller 29/2, 38, 40/1/2,
41, 51/2, 55/2, 56/1/2, 106/2; Sergio Piumatti 107; Mark Read 9;
Alessandra Santarelli 23/1, 30/2, 36/1/2, 47/1/2, 82/1/2, 116
Cover picture by: Jon Arnold
Picture Editor: Hilary Genin
Maps: Maria Randall

Editorial Director: Brian Bell
Managing Editor: Clare Peel

CONTACTING THE EDITORS: As every effort is made to provide accurate information in this publication, we would appreciate it if readers would call our
attention to any errors and omissions by contacting:
Apa Publications, PO Box 7910, London SE1 1WE, England.
Fax: (44 20) 7403 0290
e-mail: insight@apaguide.co.uk

Information has been obtained from sources believed to be reliable,
but its accuracy and completeness, and the opinions based thereon,
are not guaranteed.

© 2003 APA Publications GmbH & Co. Verlag KG Singapore Branch, Singapore.

First Edition 1995; Second Edition 2003
Printed in Singapore by Insight Print Services (Pte) Ltd
Original edition © Polyglott-Verlag Dr Bolte KG, Munich

Worldwide distribution enquiries:
APA Publications GmbH & Co. Verlag KG (Singapore Branch)
38 Joo Koon Road, Singapore 628990
Tel: (65) 6865-1600, Fax: (65) 6861-6438

Distributed in the UK & Ireland by:
GeoCenter International Ltd
The Viables Centre, Harrow Way, Basingstoke,
Hampshire RG22 4BJ
Tel: (44 1256) 817987, Fax: (44 1256) 817-988

Distributed in the United States by:
Langenscheidt Publishers, Inc.
46–35 54th Road, Maspeth, NY 11378
Tel: (1 718) 784-0055, Fax: (1 718) 784-0640

www.insightguides.com

Milan

Introduction

Places

Culture

Travel Tips

▷ **Galleria Vittorio Emanuele II (p22)**
Shop in style at this elegant city-centre arcade.

◁ **The Duomo (p16)**
At the heart of Milan is the Duomo, the third-largest church in Christendom.

▽ **Sant'Ambrogio (p63)**
This austere basilica is named after St Ambrose, the patron saint of Milan.

△ **Castello Sforzesco (p49)** Milan's castle houses a museum and art gallery.

▷ **The Navigli (p84)**
The city's canal district is one of the best areas to go in the evening.

◁ *The Last Supper* **(p60)** Leonardo's celebrated fresco, depicting Christ and his Apostles at the Last Supper, can be viewed on the wall of the Refectory adjacent to Santa Maria delle Grazie church.

△ **Pinacoteca di Brera (p36)** Tucked away in the bohemian but enduringly stylish Brera district is this wonderful art collection, a major showcase for Lombard art.

▷ **Teatro alla Scala (p28)** One of the world's top opera houses.

▽ **Palazzo Reale (p23)** The royal palace is now home to a modern art gallery and a museum about the Duomo.

▽ **The Fashion District (p78)** The main couture names that have set Milan firmly on the fashion map can be found on vias Montenapoleone, Mazoni, della Spiga and Sant'Andrea.

Milan – the Secret Capital

The Italians call it their 'secret capital', *la capitale morale*. Milan *(Milano)*, is Italy's second largest city and its main industrial and financial metropolis, the city that not only possesses the country's finest shops and its most spectacular churches, but also some of its ugliest slums. Milan owes its growth and prosperity to its wholly favourable location in the Po Basin; this is where a number of important transalpine roads meet the traffic network of the southern Alpine foothills, between the Po, Adda and Ticino rivers. The city's position is reflected in its name, which has its roots in the Latin *Mediolanum* (in the middle of the plain). In late antiquity, the Roman Empire was partly governed from Milan. In the Middle Ages the city was the springboard for conquests of Italy, and right up to modern times the surrounding plain was the stage on which 'the people of Europe settled their scores by the sword'. Today, Milan is a melting-pot for individuals who have come here in search of work, not only from all parts of Italy, but also from abroad, particularly from Africa.

RICH CULTURE

Milan is not only one of the largest cities in Italy, it is also one of the most vivacious and elegant. Since life here has revolved around progress and modernity, and the earning and spending of money, it has acquired the reputation of being a 'non-Italian', rather 'northern' city. However, Milan is far more than just a trading centre with a centuries-old tradition; it is also one of the country's most important cities of art and a significant hub of contemporary culture. Visitors are unlikely to tire of Milan: apart from the sheer inexhaustible choice of shopping, there are many fine historical sights – art collections, churches and palaces – as well as lively cultural events. This noisy, bustling metropolis, which is generally much maligned, contains some delightful and unexpectedly peaceful corners.

Opposite: the spindly spires of the Duomo
Below: Villa Reale shutters
Bottom: Milanese tram

The city's environs are also worth closer inspection, since they are home to a multitude of castles and attractions such as the towns of Bergamo and Monza, the University town of Pavia, with its Carthusian monastery, and spectacular lakes – including Como and Maggiore – all little more than an hour's drive away.

POSITION

Milan enjoys an enviable and highly fortuitous location. It lies between 100 and 145m (330 to 480ft) above sea level, not far from the River Po and the Alps, on the gently south-sloping Po Basin between two small rivers: Olona in the west and Lambro in the east. The city is connected to the Northern Italian lakes and the large rivers of the Po Basin by shipping canals *(navigli)*: to Lake Maggiore by the Naviglio Grande; the Po River by the Naviglio Pavese, and the Adda River and Lake Como by the Naviglio della Martesana.

SIZE AND POPULATION

The city of Milan covers an area of around 180sq km (70sq miles) and has a circumference of around 95km (60 miles). With a population

Crossing Piazza Mercanti

of close to 1.5 million, it is the second-largest city in Italy and occupies 10th place in the European city league. With its 35 suburbs, Greater Milan has a population of almost 4 million, and the population density is 1,900 per sq km.

Many people consider Milan to be the only truly cosmopolitan city in Italy; a genuine melting-pot with a large immigrant population. This hasn't always meant life has been easy, with clashes occuring between locals and immigrants both in the suburbs and the city centre. But history has shown that Milan has always understood how to learn from its immigrants, and there are hopes that these new citizens are gradually becoming better integrated.

There's an old expression, *El milanès el ga el cör in man*, which roughly translates as 'the Milanese wears his heart on his sleeve'. The Italians generally see the Milanese as an honest, forthright bunch, refreshingly no-nonsense and reliable. A visitor who is open to new ideas and experiences will discover an equally open and many-sided Milan.

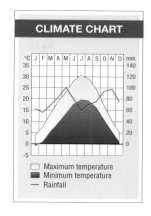

CLIMATE

Like the whole of the Po Basin, Milan has a continental climate, with fairly harsh winters and hot, muggy summers. The weather can change fairly rapidly, meaning that on any one day, temperature variations can be considerable. The best times to visit are the spring and autumn, when the average temperatures lie between 15–19°C (59–66°F). During the summer the city bakes in temperatures of around 30°C (86°F), with little shade available. Precipitation is generally quite high, and snow often falls in winter. Like many other areas of the Po Plain, Milan can also get very misty in winter, with fogs lasting up to two or three weeks.

ECONOMY

Milan, with its superior banking infrastructure, is Italy's centre of high finance and of economic and industrial power. It is also the headquarters of the country's independant television stations, its press

Milanese couture

and advertising agencies, its couture houses and many of Italy's top industrial designers. In addition, the city also possesses a number of Italy's best higher education establishments.

Fiera Milano (the Great Milan Fair) is something of a misnomer since the trade fair centre hosts fairs for most of the year. With July, August and December the only quiet months, the busiest times are spring and autumn, from a fair on tourism in February to fashion shows in March, furniture exhibitions in April, and technology, fashion and shoe fairs in September and October. (Milan's booming economy means that hotel rooms may be hard to find during fairs.)

And it isn't simply the city itself that enjoys booming business. Lombardy, the Milanese hinterland, is the richest region in the country, producing a quarter of the GNP and a third of all Italy's exports. It is the most populous region in the country and the average income of its inhabitants is double that of people in the south. The Po Plain is one of the most agriculturally fertile areas in Italy, with cereals and fodder predominating; there is also cattle farming and fruit production in the area.

ADMINISTRATION

Milan is the capital of the province of the same name and also the capital of the Italian region of

Below: inside the Galleria Vittorio Emanuele II
Bottom: Milanese businesspeople

Lombardy. The city is the seat of an archbishop, a court of appeal, transport and financial authorities, countless chambers of commerce and consulates. It has three universities (state, Catholic and commercial, with the country's most important business school, Bocconi), a polytechnic and academies of music and art.

CITY LAYOUT

It is still possible to recognise the square core of the original Roman settlement at the Piazza di San Sepolcro. The oval plan of the medieval city is today marked by the broad inner ring road, which runs from Castello Sforzesco in the northwest round to the hospital district in the southeast. This encloses most of the city's sights. The fortifications built while the city was under Spanish rule in the 16th century mark the extent to which Milan had expanded by the end of the Middle Ages.

These fortifications now lie buried beneath the central ring of main roads (the so-called *convallazione interna*). After further growth in the 19th century due to industrialisation, which extended the city's borders to the canal ring *(Cerchia dei Navigli)* and the outermost ring road *(Circonvallazione esterna)*, Milan is now expanding primarily towards the north, where many of Italy's biggest companies have relocated, creating their own infrastructure in the process. IBM, for example, has settled in Segrate to the northwest of the city.

Likewise, clusters of satellite towns have sprung up to the south – something that is less the result of planning initiatives than of property speculation. They are still outside the public transport network, and are connected to the city centre by expressways.

Since the destruction inflicted by Allied bombing raids in World War II, the city has been substantially modernised. But, in the city centre, around the magnificent Duomo, there are still a large number of classical buildings, and there's the sense of an older Milan, enhanced by an ongoing programme of restoration and renovation.

Sant'Ambrogio

Patron saint of Milan and the city's first bishop Sant' Ambrogio (St Ambrose) is thought to have been born *circa* 340 in Trier. Despite not being baptised, he reigned as bishop of Milan from 374 to 397, and his eloquent preaching is believed to have spurred on the conversion of St Augustine. He won great popularity among the Milanese, and is still remembered on his feast day – 7 December – when the La Scala opera season begins and other festivities are held across the city.

Popular form of transport

HISTORICAL HIGHLIGHTS

6th century BC Milan is founded by the Umbrian Etruscans.

396BC The settlement is overrun in an attack by the Celtic tribe of the Insubres.

222BC Milan is taken by Rome.

AD286–402 Milan becomes the capital of the Western Roman Empire, a state that is maintained until AD402.

313 In the Milan Edict of Tolerance, Emperor Constantine grants the Christians religious freedom.

374 The governor of Emilia-Liguria, Aurelius Ambrosius (later St Ambrose, or Sant'Ambrogio) is elected Bishop of Milan, despite not being baptised.

452 Attila conquers the Po Basin and Milan, which enters a period of decline.

476 The Western Roman Empire falls to the Goths. In 553 the Ostrogoths succumb to the Byzantine Emperor Justinian.

568–84 Under King Alboin I the Lombards invade Northern Italy. In 569 most of Milan's population flees before the cruel attacks of the king, who makes Pavia his residence. In 584 the Milanese return to their city, now in the hands of the kinder King Authari and his spouse, Theodolinda of Bavaria. In Monza the queen founds the first Lombard Catholic church.

773–887 Charlemagne conquers the Lombard kingdom. After his Frankish Empire is divided among his grandsons (843), Lombardy first falls to Lothair I and then (881–7) to Charles III.

888 The weak rule of the late Carolingians allows local princes to emerge. Internal fighting follows.

962 Responding to a call for help from the Papal States, the German King Otto I conquers Northern Italy. At the end of the 10th century, however, the prosperous towns of Northern Italy cast aside their ruling German princes. A struggle ensues between the Ghibellines (followers of the German emperor) and the Guelphs (supporters of the Pope).

1097 The birth of the *Comune di Milano*, the Free City of Milan, with its own independent charter.

1152 Milan is captured by Barbarossa.

1176 The Lombard League, founded in 1167, composed of the cities of Upper Italy and led by Milan, defeats Barbarossa near Legnano.

1262 Ottone Visconti becomes archbishop of Milan. Internal power struggles end with the destruction of the free communes and lead to the installation of the Signoria, the 'rule of tyranny'.

1311 Matteo Visconti becomes the uncontested ruler of Milan.

1395 Gian Galeazzo Visconti becomes Duke of Milan.

1447 After the death of Filippo Maria Visconti, the Aurea Republica Ambrosiana, a short-lived democracy, is established.

1450 The condottiere Francesco Sforza, the son-in-law of the last Visconti, becomes Duke of Milan. Another Golden Age ensues, especially during the reign of Lodovico il Moro (1479–99).

1499 Because of his blood ties with the Viscontis, Louis XII of France claims Milan for himself and conquers the city. In 1512, the Sforza return, but only briefly.

1525 Having rid Milan of the Sforzas, François I of France tries to conquer North Italy. He is defeated by Charles V.

1540 Charles V bequeaths the Duchy of Milan to his son, later Philip II of Spain. With the division of the Habsburg Empire in 1556, Milan falls to Spain and remains under Spanish rule until 1714.

1560 Carlo Borromeo (canonised in 1610) becomes Archbishop of Milan.

1701–14 The War of the Spanish Succession, with Austria, Prussia, England, Holland and Portugal on one side, and Louis XIV allied with Bavaria on the other. At the end of the war, Milan falls to Austria, which maintains its rule over the city with only short breaks until 1859.

1796 During the Wars of the Coalitions, Napoleon Bonaparte conquers Lombardy. In 1797 he creates the Cisalpine Republic, with Milan as its capital.

1802 Napoleon makes himself president of the Italian Republic that has emerged from the Cisalpine Republic. In 1805 he is crowned king of Italy in Milan.

1814–15 After the fall of Napoleon, the Congress of Vienna reaffirms Austria's claims to Lombardy.

1848 With the support of the Sardinian Royal House, the leaders of the Italian Unity Movement (Risorgimento) oust the Austrians; the latter win Milan back at the Battle of Custoza on 6 August.

1859 Austria declares war on Sardinia, which is allied with Napoleon II. After defeats at Magenta and Solferino, Austria hands Lombardy to Sardinia.

1861 Vittorio Emanuele II becomes king of Italy. Rome is pronounced capital of the new kingdom.

1900 Umberto I is murdered in Monza.

1922 From Milan, Benito Mussolini begins his March on Rome.

1945 On 27 April, while fleeing to Switzerland, Mussolini is shot at Tremezzo on Lake Como.

1946 Italy becomes a republic.

1992–5 *Mani Pulite* (Clean Hands) campaign. When a Milanese businessman refuses to pay a bribe to a local politician, the city's magistrate Antonio Di Pietro dares to investigate; the corrupt post-war order of Italian politics collapses.

1994 National elections usher in a new Italian Republic, an electoral system along British 'first-past-the-post' lines.

1994 Fashion designer Maurizio Gucci is murdered in Milan.

1996 Italy run by its first centre-left government. Romano Prodi is the new Premier. He resigns in 1998 after a vote of no confidence.

1997 Fashion giant Gianni Versace is murdered. Playwright Dario Fo, born in Parabiago in the Milan Province, wins the Nobel Prize for Literature.

1990–2001 Malpensa airport is revamped and reorganised.

2000 Major celebrations take place to welcome in the new millennium.

2001 Media magnate Silvio Berlusconi is elected Prime Minister.

2002 The euro replaces the Lira. Italy sees its first general stike for 20 years.

2003 The exiled Italian Royal family are allowed to return to Italy.

Map on page 19

Preceding pages: Galleria Vittorio Emanuele II from Piazza del Duomo
Below: the Duomo
Bottom: interior of the Duomo from the Choir

1: The Duomo and Proximity

Any first-time visitor to Milan should start at the geographical, historical and religious centre of the city; the Duomo (cathedral). You should allow at least a couple of hours for visiting the interior of the building and its roof terraces, from which there are wonderful views across the city and beyond. Just a stone's throw from the Duomo is another of Milan's main attractions: the Galleria Vittorio Emanuele II, an imposing glass-roofed arcade and home to Milanese fashion giant, Prada. If time allows, there are two major museums in this area: the Museo del Duomo (Cathedral Museum) and the Civico Museo d'Arte Contemporanea (CIMAC), or Contemporary Art Museum, housed in Palazzo Reale, the former royal palace, adjacent to the Duomo.

THE DUOMO

Milan's magnificent ★★★ **Duomo** ❶ (open daily 6.45am–6.45pm; note that you will not be allowed in if you're wearing shorts, a mini skirt or if your shoulders are uncovered) is the city's greatest attraction and the third-largest church in Christendom (after Rome's St Peter's and the cathedral in Seville). Even if stylistically speaking it is not as pure as some of its counterparts in France – a

fact explained by its lengthy building time – the Duomo impresses because of its massive dimensions and elegant proportions. It is the best example of Gothic architecture in Italy and also demonstrates more clearly than any other building the conflict between the vernacular Lombard and northern Gothic styles: the Italian Gothic is manifested in the vast width of the edifice, while the northern Gothic is evident in the flying buttresses and the upward-striving forms typical of French cathedrals.

Star Attraction
● **the Duomo**

CONSTRUCTION

Work on the Duomo began in 1386 under the patronage of Bishop Antonio da Saluzzo. It is not known who drew up the plans, but it is presumed that they were the combined effort of several Lombard master builders who had learned their trade working on the great cathedral in Cologne. In the early years the supervision of the building lay in the hands of Italian, French and German architects, who replaced one another in rapid succession.

Detail of the Duomo's front door

Arguments between the foreign and local masters ended in 1400 with the appointment of Filippino degli Organi as supervisor, and in 1418 the high altar was ready to be consecrated by Pope Martin V. Towards the end of the 15th century, building was supervised by Guiniforte Solari and Giovanni Antonio Amadeo, two architects influenced by the Renaissance. In 1499 work was interrupted for a while owing to the death of Lodovico il Moro; after Amadeo passed away in 1522, progress came to a complete standstill.

It was only during the time of Cardinal Carlo Borromeo that work on the Duomo was resumed. In 1567 Pellegrino Tibaldi was entrusted with continuing the project and drew up designs, according to the tastes of the time, for a magnificent Baroque façade that stood in complete contrast to the rest of the building. In 1572 Carlo Borromeo consecrated the church to the memory of the birth of the Virgin Mary. Tibaldi's façade was begun in 1616, but it was later transformed into Gothic style and remained incomplete. Work

Map on page 19

👁 **Lavish exterior**
The building is faced in white marble from quarries north of Lago Maggiore. Some 135 tracery elements, as well as 2,245 statues and 96 atlases for supporting the gargoyles decorate the roof and exterior surfaces.

The Madonnina

on the exterior continued during the 18th and 19th centuries: between 1805–13 Napoleon I had the west façade completed according to the plans of Carlo Amati, and this period also saw the completion of the decorative elements. Additions to the upper parts of the building date from the early 20th century, and further work on the portals was carried out between 1948 and 1950.

To give some idea of the immensity of the Duomo, it measures 158m (520ft) long and 66m (215ft) wide; the central nave is 17m (55ft) wide and 48m (157ft) high; and the interior height of the cupola is 68m (220ft). The main façade is 61m (200ft) wide and 56m (180ft) high. It is said that the cathedral can house up to 40,000 people.

THE MAIN FAÇADE

The main façade, although breathtaking, is the least harmonious part of the building because it reflects the variety of styles that succeeded each other during the course of its long period of construction. The lower half, with the classical-baroque elements by Pellegrino Tibaldi (16th century), stands in complete contrast to the Gothic forms of Carlo Buzzi on the upper half of the structure; something that is very evident in the differing shapes of the windows.

The plinths of the six massive vertical buttresses that divide the façade into five sections are decorated with reliefs depicting biblical stories, as well as supporting figures (17th–18th century). On the pillar consoles there are statues of the Apostles and Prophets, added in the 19th century.

The early baroque portal surrounds are by Tibaldi, while the massive bronze doors date from the 20th century. With the exception of the central doorway, the designs embellishing them are all of Milanese motifs.

THE INTERIOR

Inside the five-naved basilica are 914 statues and 52 composite pillars; one for each week of the year. The capitals atop the pillars date mostly

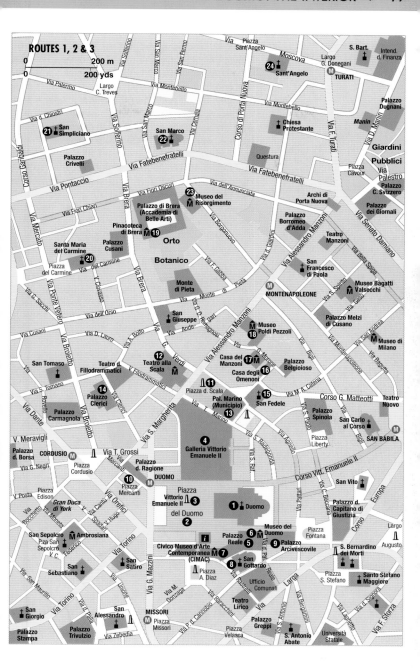

ROUTES 1, 2 & 3

0 ———————— 200 m
0 ———————— 200 yds

Via Palermo

Largo
C. Treves

Via Montebello

Via d. Chiostri

Via Solferino

Via San Marco

Via San Fermo

Via San Marco

Piazza
Sant'Angelo

Via
Sant'Angelo

Moscova

Largo
G. Donegani

S. Bart.

Intend.
d. Finanza

24 Sant'Angelo

TURATI

Via Montebello

Corso di Porta Nuova

Via Montebello

Palazzo
Dugnani

Chiesa
Protestante

Manin

Via T. Turati

Via Manin

21 San
Simpliciano

San Marco

22

Via Cernaia

Giardini

Questura

Pubblici

Via Fatebenefratelli

Via Pontaccio

Palazzo
Crivelli

Via Fatebenefratelli

Via dell'Annunciata

Piazza
Cavour

Via
Palestro

Corso Garibaldi

Corso Como

Via Fiori Oscuri

23 Museo del
Risorgimento

Archi di
Porta Nuova

Palazzo
C. Svizzero

Via Fiori Chiari

Palazzo di Brera
(Accademia di
Belle Arti)

Via Brera

Palazzo
Borromeo
d'Adda

Palazzo
dei Giornali

Via Senato

Via Mercato

Pinacoteca
di Brera

19

Palazzo
Cusani

Orto

Teatro
Manzoni

Via Damiani

Santa Maria
del Carmine

20

Botanico

San
Francesco
di Paola

Piazza
del Carmine

Via del Carmine

Via F. Gabba

Via A. Manzoni

Museo Bagatti
Valsecchi

Via G. Sacchi

V. Ciovasso

Via Brera

Monte
di Pieta

Via Monte

Via Pietà

MONTENAPOLEONE

Via S. Spirito

Via Gesù

Palazzo
Melzi
di Cusano

Via Ponte Vetero

Via dell'Orso

San
Giuseppe

Via A. Boito

Via D. Lauro

Via Andegari

Verdi

Via S. Andrea

Museo di
Milano

San Tomaso

18 Museo
Poldi Pezzoli

Via Montenapoleone

Via Cusani

Teatro
Fillodrammatici

Via S. Tomaso

12 Teatro alla
Scala

Via Filodrammatici

Casa del
Manzoni

17

Via A. Morone

Casa degli
Omenoni

Palazzo
Belgioioso

Via Bigli

Via Boschetti

Via Dante

14

Palazzo
Clerici

11

Piazza d. Scala

15

Corso G. Matteotti

Teatro
Nuovo

Via Clerici

Via S. Margherita

16

Via M.A. Catena

Palazzo
Carmagnola

Via Broletto

Pal. Marino
(Municipio)

13

San Fedele

Palazzo
Spinola

Via S. Paolo

San Carlo
al Corso

V. Meravigli

Via T. Grossi

4 Galleria Vittorio
Emanuele II

Via I. Marino

Via S. Radegonda

Piazza
Liberty

SAN BABILA

Palazzo
d. Borsa

CORDUSIO

Via G. Negri

Piazza
Cordusio

Via Mercanti

Palazzo
d. Ragione

DUOMO

Piazza

Corso Vitt. Emanuele II

Via S. Raffaele

Via Agnello

Europa

Piazza
Edison

V. Posta

10

Piazza
Mercanti

Vittorio
Emanuele II

3

Via Orefici

Piazza
del Duomo

2

1 Duomo

Palazzo d.
Capitano di
Giustizia

San Vito

Via C. Beccaria

Gran Duca
di York

Via Cantù

Via Unione

Museo del
Duomo

6

Piazza
Fontana

Largo
Augusto

San Sepolcro

Ambrosiana

Via Spadari

Pza San
Sepolcro
V. C.

Federico

Civico Museo d'Arte
Contemporanea
(CIMAC)

i

Palazzo
Reale

7

5

9

Palazzo
Arcivescovile

S. Bernardino
dei Morti

San
Sebastiano

San
Satiro

Via G. Mazzini

8

San
Gottardo

Piazza
Diaz

Via Rastrelli

Via d. Pattari

Largo

Via A. Corso

Piazza
S. Stefano

Santo Stefano
Maggiore

Via San Maurilio

San Giorgio

San
Alessandro

Via Unione

Teatro
Lirico

Ufficio
Comunali

Via Larga

Via S. Antonio

Via A. Signorelli

Palazzo
Stampa

Palazzo
Trivulzio

Via Zebedia

MISSORI

Piazza
Missori

Via P. d. Cannobio

Piazza
Velasca

Palazzo
Greppi

S. Antonio
Abate

Università
Statale

Via F. Sforza

Via Torino

Via S. Antonio

Via Laghetto

Map on page 19

The Madonnina
Between 1765 and 1769 the main spire of the Duomo was added; in 1774 it was topped with the 4-m (14-ft) golden statue of the Virgin, or the Madonnina, as she is known. The top of the crossing tower with the crowning statue of the Madonnina is a lofty 110m (355ft) above the ground. She is considered to be the city protector.

from 1410–50, and their rich decoration of figures of the saints is mainly the work of Filippino da Modena. The marble mosaic floor was designed by Tibaldi.

For a detailed tour of the interior and information on the history of each of the windows, side altars and statues, it's worth paying the small fee for an audioguide (available just inside the main entrance). If you intend to focus on the highlights of the Duomo, look out, in the southeastern corner, for a gruesome ★★ **statue of St Bartholomew being flayed alive**, which dates from 1562. The sculpture bears the boastful inscription 'It wasn't Praxiteles, but Marco d'Agrate that made me.'

Along the northern edge of the Duomo is the celebrated ★★ **Trivulzio Candelabrum**. This seven-armed, 5-m (16-ft) high bronze candle holder is a magnificent example of French art of the late 12th century and is thought to be the work of the goldsmith Nicolas de Verdun; in 1562 it was donated to the Duomo by the priest Giambattista Trivulzio.

The jewel in the Duomo's crown, however, is the ★★ **Holy Nail of the Cross**, believed to have come from the True Cross. The relic is stored in a niche in the vault way up above the choir, and

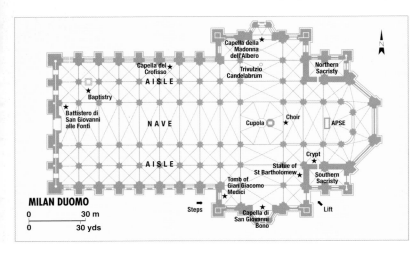

MILAN DUOMO

Capella della Madonna dell'Albero ★

Capella del ★ Crofisso

Trivulzio Candelabrum

AISLE

Northern Sacristy

★ Baptistry

Battistero di San Giovanni alle Fonti ★

NAVE

Cupola ○

Choir ★

APSE

AISLE

Crypt ★

Statue of St Bartholomew ★

Southern Sacristy

Tomb of Gian Giacomo Medici ★

Steps →

Capella di San Giovanni Bono ★

↘ Lift

0   30 m
0   30 yds

each year, on 14 September, the Bishop of Milan is hoisted up to the niche on pulleys, so that he can show the nail to the public below.

Also of particular note, is the apse, at the eastern end of the building, since this is the oldest part of the cathedral. Constructed in pre-Gothic style, it has three massive lancet windows, which date from *circa* 1390 and are the work of Nicolas de Bonaventura, with delicated tracery by Filippino degli Organi. These are the largest lancet windows in the world.

THE ROOF TERRACES

The Duomo's broad ★★ **roof terraces** *(le terraze;* Mar–Oct 9am–5.45pm, Nov–Feb 9am–4.15pm) are faced with marble slabs and lead all the way round the building, providing fabulous views over Milan and its outlying mountains. From the terraces, visitors can examine close up some of the Duomo's details, such as the flying buttresses, gables, pinnacles, spires and statues.

The terraces can be reached by taking a lift at the northeast side of the cathedral. The entrance is on the outside. There are quite a few steps to climb at the top of the lift, so it's advisable to wear comfortable, flat shoes.

The 14th-century *Guglia Carelli*, the Duomo's oldest gable, is worthy of special attention; located above the corner pilaster of the northern sacristy, it faces the Corso Vittorio Emanuele II, which runs along the north side of the cathedral, and is named after its donor, Marco Carelli. For notable statuary, look out for the 16th-century *Eve* (Solari school), to the south of the apse, and *Adam,* on its northern side.

PIAZZA DEL DUOMO

In front of the Duomo is **Piazza del Duomo ❷**, which was given its present-day appearance between 1862 and 1878 by the architect Giuseppe Mengoni. Along the long sides of the once-modest square he constructed the two blocks of buildings with colonnades: Palazzo Meridionale

Star Attractions
- **St Bartholomew statue**
- **Trivulzio Candelabrum**
- **Holy Nail of the Cross**
- **the roof terraces**

Below: apse windows
Bottom: Monument to Vittorio Emanuele II, Piazza del Duomo

Map on page 19

Galleria particulars

The gallery's arcades are 197m (645ft) and 105m (345ft) long, with a width of 14.5m (47ft) and height of 26m (85ft); the glass dome measures 39m (127ft) in diameter. Mosaics on the lunettes show the continents of Africa, America, Asia and Europe, while those on the floor depict the coats-of-arms of Vittorio Emanuele's family and the symbols of Milan (a red cross on a white ground), Turin (a bull), Rome (a she-wolf) and Florence (a lily).

Roof detail, Galleria Vittorio Emanuele II

in the south and, in the north, Palazzo Settentrionale, which is crowned by the imposing entrance to the Galleria Vittorio Emanuele II *(see below)*. Opposite the cathedral, the square is completed by the Palazzo dell'Orologio.

In the middle of Piazza del Duomo stands the **monument to Vittorio Emanuele II** ❸, sculpted in 1896 by Ercole Rosa. The bronze equestrian statue shows the king at the battle of San Martino (1859); the reliefs on the plinth depict the entry of French-Piedmontese troops into Milan after the battle of Magenta (1859).

GALLERIA VITTORIO EMANUELE II

Along the north side of Piazza del Duomo is the glorious ★★ **Galleria Vittorio Emanuele II** ❹. This monumental complex of intersecting arcades forms the link between Piazza del Duomo and Piazza della Scala. It is often referred to as the Salon of Milan, because, with its elegant cafés and shops, it is the place where the Milanese traditionally converge. Built in Renaissance style between 1865 and 1867 according to the plans of architect Giuseppe Mengoni, the Galleria was one of the earliest buildings to use cast iron and glass in its construction. Tragically, the architect plunged to his death from scaffolding on the building, just days before it was inaugurated in

1867 by the recently crowned king after whom the gallery is named. In 1878, a 38.5-m (125-ft) high triumphal arch facing the Duomo was added. Nowadays, the gallery is still home to Milanese institutions such as café-restaurant Savini *(see page 115)*, a large branch of fashion house Prada, a major branch of Rizzoli booksellers and, unfortunately, several less traditional chains such as McDonald's and Levi's.

PALAZZO REALE

Immediately to the southeast of Piazza del Duomo is a smaller square – Piazzetta Reale – and the neoclassical ★★ **Palazzo Reale ❺**. In the 11th and 12th centuries this was the site of the Broletto Vecchio, Milan's old town hall, which became the residence of the Viscontis in the early 14th century. Between 1330 and 1336 Azzone Visconti had the building converted into the magnificent Corte Ducale Visconte (Ducal Court of the Viscontis). The palace lost its importance when its front part was removed to make way for the Duomo, and when in 1385 the Viscontis moved into the Castello Sforzesco *(see page 49)*. Between the 16th and 17th centuries, when the remainder of the building became the residence of the Spanish governor, the former courtyard (today's Piazzetta Reale) served as the ceremonial entrance. In the 18th century this was the location of Milan's very first opera house.

The palace was given its present neoclassical countenance between 1771 and 1778 when it became the residence of the Austrian Archduke Ferdinand; the radical alterations were carried out under the direction of Giuseppe Piermarini. After the unification of Italy (1861), the building was named the Royal Palace.

MUSEO DEL DUOMO

A side wing of the Palazzo Reale houses the **Museo del Duomo ❻** (Piazza Duomo 14; open daily 10am–1.15pm and 3–6pm), home to cathedral artefacts dating from the 14th to 19th

Below: Prada, Milan
Bottom: the symbol of the city

Map on page 19

Stained glass from the Duomo

CARD. A.C FERRARI

centuries and showcase for the history of the great edifice. The following is a room-by-room breakdown of the main exhibits.

In the entrance hall (Room 1) is photography of the Duomo as well as marble plaques with the trademark of the 'Honourable Cathedral Construction Site' (explanations only in Italian). In pride of place in Room 2 is *St Agnes* (1491, by Benedetto Briosco), while to the right are three 14th-century marble statues that previously stood on the Carelli-Fiale. Also in this room are the original cast of the *Madonnina*, (the Virgin, 1769, by Perego), a number of Flemish works, including the 16th-century *Deposition*, and reproductions of drawings of the Duomo's construction, notably works by Leonardo da Vinci.

In the centre of Room 3 is *St George* (1404, by Georgio Solari), which blatantly displays the facial features of Gian Galeazzo Visconti. Also here are various mouldings of 15th-century gargoyles, *Warrior in Armour* (1404, by Matteo Raverti) and *Titan* (15th century, German school).

Moving on to Room 4, you'll see a plaster cast of the monument to Pope Martin V. In the middle of the room is *St Paul the Hermit* (*circa* 1470, by Cristoforo Mantegazza).

Now continue to Room 6, where there are terracotta studies from the 17th and 18th centuries, a 15th-century *St Sebastian* and two 16th-century Gobelins tapestries depicting scenes from the Old Testament. In the middle of the hall is the 15th-century *Jonah*, by Cristoforo Solari and *Joshua* (late 15th century).

Next is Room 7, where on the entrance corbels are *Jesus* and *Mary* (both 15th century); on the walls there are 17th-century terracotta studies for the Duomo's façade reliefs and, above them, the matching distemper paintings by G.B. Crespi. In the middle of the room is another *St Sebastian* (15th century, Lombard), *St Agapitus at the Stake* (1607, by Andrea Biffi) and *Disputation of the Doctors of the Church*, executed in the late 16th century and an early work by Tintoretto.

Further exhibits from the 15th to 17th centuries are on display in Rooms 8 and 9. In the centre of room 10 is a wooden model of the Duomo, dating from *circa* 1520. Other models of various façade designs are also on show here, notably one by Giuseppe Brentano that dates from 1888 and was awarded first prize in an international competition; the design was never realised, however.

At the centre of Room 11 is a bronze model of the main spire of the Duomo; further designs for the façade can also be seen here.

In Room 12 you can see pieces of marble from the quarries of Candoglia, which provided the building material for the cathedral from 1386; also on show here are mouldings of portal reliefs.

CIVICO MUSEO D'ARTE CONTEMPORANEA

The second floor of the Palazzo Reale is home to part of the collection of the ★ **Civico Museo d'Arte Contemporanea (CIMAC)** ❼ (galleries open Tues–Sun 9.30am–5.30pm), a superb summary of the works of European artists from the end of the 19th century to the present day. The collection consists partly of art that was obtained during the course of the 20th century and partly of paintings donated by the collectors Ausonio Canavese (including works by the Futurist, Umberto Boccioni) and Antonio Boschi, as well as from the artists Fontana and Melotti. Strong

Contemporary art
Following major refurbishment at CIMAC, the gallery's contemporary art collection (in this case, work produced since the 1990s) is on show at the Museo del Presente (Officine del gas di Bovisa, Via Giampietrino 24; Metro: Bovisa), an immense converted gasworks in the northern suburb of Bovisa. This major addition to the Milanese art scene will feature temporary exhibitions by up-and-coming European artists and works designed particularly for this space.

Palazzo Reale, home to CIMAC, from the roof of the Duomo

Map on page 19

Below: San Gottardo al Palazzo
Bottom: Palazzo Arcivescovile

emphasis is also given to the Futurists and abstract artists, with works by Gino Rossi, Modigliani, Savinio, de Chirico, Severini, and Morandi, as well as the *Corrente* artists and the Lombard *Chiarismo*. The Jucker Collection is also on show here, as are changing contemporary exhibitions.

SAN GOTTARDO AL PALAZZO

The Palazzo Reale complex also contains the former ducal chapel of **San Gottardo al Palazzo ❽** (entrance in Via Pecorari; Mon–Fri 8am–noon and 2–6pm, Sat 8am–4pm, Sun 8am–1pm). It was built in 1336 by Francesco Pecorari and, like the Palazzo Reale, was redesigned in 1770 in the neoclassical style by Piermarini. Remains of the Gothic era include the entrance portal and the elegant octagonal bell tower, crowned with the gilded statue of St Michael. The warm brick tones of the tower form a stunning contrast to the white of the columns at its top. The unusual apse, which has gable windows and a dwarf gallery (an arcaded wall-passage on the outside of the building), dates from the 14th century and is from an even earlier building.

Inside the chapel, to the left of the high altar, is the barely intact tomb of the donor of the church, Azzone Visconti; the tomb is the work of Giovanni di Balduccio and was produced during the 14th century; the 17th-century fresco opposite, the work of Cerano, shows Carlo Borromeo. On the rear wall of the nave a fragment of the Giotto school fresco *Crucifixion* has been preserved.

PALAZZO ARCIVESCOVILE

The next place to visit on this route is the **Palazzo Arcivescovile ❾**, the Archbishop's Palace. First built in 1170, it was transformed and extended several times during the following centuries, particularly during the tenure in the 16th century of Cardinal Carlo Borromeo, by the architect Pellegrino Tibaldi. The façade facing eastwards towards Piazza Fontana (1784–1801) was the work of Piermarini, who was also responsible for the large fountain in the middle of the square (from here there is a great view of the Duomo's spires). The doorway in the façade leads through to a cloister, which gives access to the Palace Chapel, also by Piermarini, and some living quarters (closed to the public).

On the north side of the palace is Via Arcivescovado. At No 6 is a large marble doorway by Tibaldi, which leads to the second of the palace's courtyards, the *Cortile della Canonica* (Canons' Courtyard), also by Tibaldi. At the centre of the courtyard, note the massive statues of *Moses* (1865, by Tantardini) and *Aaron* (1864, by Strazzo).

PIAZZA MERCANTI

On the far western side of Piazza Duomo is a delightful corner of medieval Milan, **Piazza Mercanti ⑩**. This was the centre of city life during the time of the free communes *(see page 12)*. The Piazza formed a closed square, from which six gates led out into the six districts that then comprised the town. In 1865, in order to facilitate traffic, Via Mercanti was extended through the square, thus robbing Piazza Mercanti of its closed character. But it's still a peaceful place, despite ongoing renovation, with a lovely 16th-century fountain in the middle and a number of notable buildings surrounding it.

Popular sayings
Italians are renowned for their deep mistrust of the State. The popular saying, *fatta la legge, trovato l'inganno*, meaning 'a law is passed, a way past is found', has now become a national motto.

Another popular saying, rather more specific to Milan, is *loungo come la fabbrica del Duomo* – the phrase means 'as long as the building of the Duomo' and is generally used to refer to anything that seems never-ending.

Milanese trams

Map on page 19

Opera musem
Previously housed on Piazza alla Scala, Milan's opera museum, the **Museo Teatrale alla Scala** has now been moved to Palazzo Busca (Corso Magenta 71), to the west of the city centre. The museum, which was originally founded in 1913, documents the history of La Scala and opera in Milan, and displays a rich collection of important opera memorabilia. Highlights include musical instruments such as a piano that belonged to Liszt, operatic costumes and masks, and busts and portraits of the great operatic composers and conductors, from paintings of Verdi and Maria Callas to Wagner's eerie death mask. The museum's specialist library is also located in Palazzo Busca.

Piazza della Scala, with a statue of Leonardo at its centre

2: Around Piazza della Scala

This second route takes you from the grandiose Milanese institution of La Scala opera house through some of the city's elegant backstreets to a fine 19th-century private art collection at the Museo Poldi Pezzoli. The tour can easily be covered in half a day.

PIAZZA DELLA SCALA

At the northern end of the Galleria Vittorio Emanuele II is the recently renovated **Piazza della Scala ⑪**, in the middle of which is a large ★ **monument to Leonardo da Vinci** and his Milanese students Boltraffio, Salaino, Marco d'Oggiono and Cesare da Sesto (1872, by Pietro Magni). The reliefs portray the different fields of work in which Leonardo was involved: painting *(Last Supper)*, anatomy (equestrian statue of Sforza), architecture (fortifications) and physics (hydraulic engineering).

LA SCALA OPERA HOUSE

The northwest side of the square is occupied by the ★★ **Teatro alla Scala ⑫** (currently closed for renovation until 2004), or 'La Scala', as the world-renowned opera house is familiarly known.

Given the prestige of the house – to have an engagement here remains the pinnacle of many performers' careers – the plain, neoclassical exterior of the building is rather disappointing. Inside, however, things are more impressive. With its 2,000 seats, La Scala is still by far the largest theatre in Europe, its large mirror-lined upstairs foyer and lush, deep-red and gold auditorium are staggeringly opulent, and the theatre's acoustics are exceptional. The opening of the opera season on the day of the city's patron saint St Ambrose (7 December) is still the greatest society event of the year in Milan.

While the extensive renovation is being carried out, performances are being held at the high-tech **Teatro degli Arcimbaldi** (Viale dell'Innovazione; Metro: Precotto then special bus), designed by Vittorio Gregotti and located in the up-and-coming Bicocca district to the north of the city. Information on ticket availability is supplied by an electronic terminal next to the ticket office at the Duomo metro station. Payment can be made in euros or by credit card. You can also telephone the Scala Infotel Service, tel: 02 720 037 44, from 9am–6pm weekdays, and buy tickets by phone on 02 860775. Tickets can also be purchased online, at www.teatroallascala.org

BACKGROUND

The existence of Milan's original opera house is principally thanks to Empress Maria Theresa. After the Teatro Regio Ducale burned down in 1776, Maria Theresa approved the plan for a new theatre, although only 'at the expense of the people of Milan' (in the end she generously covered most of the costs herself). Constructed in understated neoclassical style by Giuseppe Piermarini, the building stands on the site of the old church of Santa Maria della Scala, which had been donated in 1385 by Regina della Scala, the wife of Bernabò Visconti – hence the name of today's opera house. The ceremonial opening took place on 3 August 1778 with a performance of *L'Europa Riconosciuta* (Europe's Recognition),

Below: detail of the Leonardo statue
Bottom: bust of Verdi

Map on page 19

an opera by the Vienna court composer Antonio Salieri; adversary of Mozart and teacher of Beethoven, Schubert and Liszt.

FROM ROSSINI TO TOSCANINI

Numerous world-class composers have cut their teeth in Milan. In 1812, the 12-year-old Gioacchino Rossini achieved his first sensational success at La Scala. In 1822 Gaetano Donizetti made his debut here, going on to write six operas for the Milanese house. In 1829 the premiere of Vincenzo Bellini's *Foreigner*, one of the greatest successes the opera house ever witnessed, was staged at La Scala. Rossini, Donizetti and Bellini dominated the scene until 1839, when the young Giuseppe Verdi came to La Scala with his work *Oberto Conte di San Bonifacio*. The Verdi era, in which the opera house reached unimaginable heights, had begun. The international success of Giacomo Puccini's tragic opera *Madame Butterfly* (his second version, the one we hear today) also started at La Scala.

Maria Callas
Inextricably linked with La Scala is diva Maria Callas (1923–77). Born in New York, to immigrant Greek parents, Callas opened the season at La Scala in 1951, to great acclaim. Over the next seven years the Milanese opera house provided a stage for her greatest triumphs. In May 1958, however, she quarrelled with the director of the house, Antonio Ghiringhelli, and decided not to sing while the house was under his control. She never performed again at La Scala.

After a short period of crisis, the arrival of Arturo Toscanini heralded an era in which the famous conductor transformed La Scala once again into one of the leading opera houses in the world. In 1943 the building was severely damaged by World War II bombs, but as early as 11 May

Palazzo Marino

1946 La Scala was reopened with a concert conducted by Toscanini. Since 1986 Neapolitan Riccardo Muti has been Musical Director at La Scala.

PALAZZO MARINO

Opposite La Scala is Milan's impressive town hall, ★ **Palazzo Marino** ⑬ (visits by appointment only, tel: 02-62085118). This boldly proportioned building was commissioned in 1558 by the Genoese Tomaso Marino, who had attained extraordinary wealth in Milan. Building work almost came to a standstill after the death of the artist Galeazzo Alessi in 1572, and the palace changed hands several times before being taken over by the city in 1861. The façade was erected between 1888 and 1890 by Luca Beltrami. The palace contains a magnificently ornamented inner courtyard, and its ground-floor Alessi Hall is lavishly decorated with stucco and paintings.

Below: San Fedele
Bottom: taking a break

PALAZZO CLERICI

Those with enough time on their hands can now progress westwards to **Palazzo Clerici** ⑭. In addition to its grandiose Hall of Mirrors and Golden Hall, this early 18th-century palazzo contains the so-called Galleria degli Arazzi (Gobelins Gallery). On the richly decorated walls hang four priceless 17th-century tapestries. Especially valuable is the ceiling fresco *Mercury Driving the Sun Chariot,* executed by the Venetian baroque painter Giambattista Tiepolo *circa* 1740. The painting depicts Mercury racing across the heavens inhabited by Olympian gods, passing en route the people and animals symbolising the continents.

SAN FEDELE

Back at Piazza alla Scala, head along Via Marino towards Piazza San Fedele, with its monument to the poet Alessandro Manzoni (1883, by Barzaghi). Beyond is the Jesuit church of **San Fedele** ⑮ (open daily 7.30am–2.30pm and 4–7pm), built between 1569 and 1579 by Pellegrino Tibaldi and

Map on page 19

Below: Casa del Manzoni
Bottom: Casa degli Omenoni

typical of 16th-century Milanese architecture. There are some beautiful paintings inside: to the right of the first altar is a *St Ignatius in Glory* (16th century, by Giovanni Battista Crespi, called Cerano) and to the right of the second altar a *Transfiguration* (1565, by Bernardino Campi). Also notable is a 16th-century *Descent from the Cross,* by Simone Petersano, the tutor of Caravaggio, to the left of the first altar. Alongside the confessionals, carved in the 16th century by Taurini, and the choir-stalls (16th century, by Anselmo del Conte) is the ★★ **Sacristy**, which is considered the most beautiful in Milan on account of its exquisitely carved cupboards (the entrance is behind the second altar on the right).

Behind the church of San Fedele is the narrow Via Omenoni, which takes its name from the eight large caryatids or Atlases (by Antonio Abbondio) on the lower half of the façade of the **Casa degli Omenoni** ⑯ (closed to the public). The celebrated sculptor Leone Leoni, called Aretino, built this house for himself in 1573. The frieze running under the cornice bears the relief *Lions Tear the Calumnition Apart.*

CASA DEL MANZONI

Situated on the adjoining Piazza Belgioioso is the striking palazzo of the same name, constructed in

1772–81 by Piermarini, and on the left the **Casa del Manzoni** (open Tues–Sun 9am–noon and 2–4pm). This was the residence of the poet Alessandro Manzoni from 1814 until 22 May 1873, when he tripped on the steps of the nearby church of San Fedele and died shortly after. The study is situated on the ground floor, while on the first floor are the dining-room, the drawing room (original furnishings from 1861, portraits of a number of Manzoni's friends including the German writer, Goethe), the bedroom in which there is a picture of the poet (1847), and the room in which Manzoni died. First editions of all Manzoni's works can be found in the gallery.

MUSEO POLDI PEZZOLI

Now follow Via Marone as far as Via Manzoni and the ★★ **Museo Poldi Pezzoli** (Via Manzoni 12; open Tues–Sun 10am–6pm). Of all the numerous private collections established in Milan by wealthy collectors during the 19th century, this one, which was left as an art foundation in 1879 by the nobleman Gian Giacomo Poldi Pezzoli (1822–79), is arguably the finest.

Alongside the paintings, the house of Giacomo Poldi Pezzoli contains a selected assortment of handicrafts, sculpture, textiles, weapons and instruments dating from Roman times onwards. The building was badly damaged during the war, but its 25 rooms were rebuilt almost exactly according to their original form and decoration.

GROUND FLOOR

Poldi Pezzoli's primary passion was collecting armour, and Room 1 is an **armoury**, containing more than 1,000 Italian, German, Spanish and Far Eastern pieces restored in the museum's workshop. Room 2 showcases frescoes, fine carpets and tapestries. The highlight here is the magnificent Persian carpet, dating from 1542–3, depicting a hunting scene.

In Room 3 is a fine collection of Italian lace from the 16th to 20th centuries, incorporating

Statue of Manzoni

Museo Poldi Pezzoli

recent private donations. Among the items on display is an Italian bedcover dating from the 17th century that once belonged to Poldi Pezzoli.

At the base of the lovely open staircase is a baroque fountain by Petiti. The staircase itself is embellished with early 18th-century landscape paintings by Magnasco and leads to the upper floor, which contains a fine painting collection.

THE LOMBARD ROOMS

On the first floor are the Lombard Rooms, which contain paintings from the Lombard School from the 15th to 16th centuries. These include: a notable *Madonna with Child* (16th century) by Vincenzo Foppa; *Nursing Mother and Flight into Egypt* (*circa* 1500) by Andrea Solario; *Madonna with Christ Child Picking Flowers* (16th century) by Boltraffio; the reputed *Mystical Wedding of St Catherine* (*circa* 1500), painted by Bernardino Luini; and a 16th-century wood carving entitled *Marriage of Mary*.

The originally rococo-style Room 7 contains terracotta, European and Oriental porcelain and majolica, largely based on the collection of Poldi Pezzoli. Most of the pieces are European, from Meissen to Vienna and Doccia to Capodimonte.

Room 8 is known as the Black Room. It derives its name from the original colour of the walls, which were lined with inlaid ebony but largely destroyed during the bombardment. Nowadays, only the wooden door, with bas reliefs showing the four seasons and day and night, remains. Exhibits include the sculpture *Faith in God* by Lorenzo Bartolini; *St Catherine of Alexandria* by Bergognone and *Artemis* by Maestro di Griselda.

Next is a bedroom (Room 9), containing portraits of Giuseppe Molteni's family and a collection of beautiful Murano glass from the 15th to 19th centuries, mostly from the collection of Poldi Pezzoli.

Room 10, the Dante Room, is the most fascinating in the house and is one of the best examples of the historicism and the neo-Gothic style that charcterised the late 19th century. Note the windows, which are painted with scenes from Dante's *Divine Comedy*.

In Room 11, the picture room, there are works on show by Pietro Lorenzetti, Cosmè Tura, Crivelli, Vitale da Bologna and Venetian painters of the 17th century, such as Guardi, Canaletto, Tiepolo and Rosalba Carriera. In Room 12 is a rich collection of gold, enamel and bronze works, as well as some porcelain.

SUNDIALS AND CLOCKS

Room 13 showcases a fine collection of over 200 sundials from the 16th to 19th centuries, while Room 14 – the Golden Room – is home to a *Mary with Child* and *Bewailing of Christ* by Botticelli, generally considered to be a poor example of his work. Also here are *St Nicola da Tolentino* by Piero della Francesca, *Portrait of a Young Woman* (*circa* 450) by Pollainolo and paintings by masters including Giovanni Bellini, Andrea Mantegna, Cosmè Tura and Vivarini.

Room 15, the Visconti Venosta Room, includes an extraordinary processional cross attributed to Raffaello Sanzio. In Room 16 are 129 valuable clocks and timepieces dating from the 16th to 19th centuries and, finally, in Room 17, are portraits by Vittore Ghislandi, P. Borroni and G. Ceruti.

The library
The Pezzoli library (Room 4) can be found on the ground floor of the building. It is home to an important and priceless collection of some 3,500 antique books from the 15th to 19th centuries including incunabula, as well as some fine illustrated manuscripts dating from the 7th and 8th centuries.

Lamentation over the Dead Christ *by Sandro Botticelli*

Map opposite

3: The Brera

This route takes you round Milan's chic, bohemian Brera district, traditionally the city's artisan area. Quiet during the day, except for activity in its handful of low-key but stylish boutiques, art galleries and cafés, the Brera picks up at night when the locals stroll along its pleasant cobbled pedestrian streets. This part of the city is also home to one of the most prestigious art collections in Italy, the Pinacoteca di Brera, and several churches that are excellent examples of the Lombard Romanesque architectural style.

Below and bottom: shopping in the Brera – one of the city's most style-conscious areas

PINACOTECA DI BRERA

The main artery through the area is Via Brera and this is where we start. At No 28 is the **Palazzo di Brera** – the present building, with its acclaimed art gallery the ★★★ **Pinacoteca di Brera** ⓳ (Via Brera 28; open Tues–Sun 8.30am–7pm), was erected for the Jesuit College according to the designs of F.M. Richini in 1651 on the site of a 12th-century monastery built outside the city for the Brothers of Mercy. After the abolition of the Jesuit Order in 1773, Maria Theresa founded Milan's Academy of Fine Arts here, the collections of which formed the basis of the Pinacoteca. The magnificent main portal (1776–84) is by Piermarini. The rooms of the gallery had to be largely rebuilt after they were struck by bombs in 1943.

Alongside the art gallery, the palace today houses the **Biblioteca Braidense**, the largest library in the city, the **Accademia di Belle Arti di Brera** (Academy of Fine Arts) and an observatory. Here you can find astronomical aparatus that was used by the observatory for two centuries. In front of the palace stands a monument to the painter Francesco Hayez (1890, by Barzaghi), who was once the director of the academy *(see box on page 43)*.

The colonnades of the beautiful two-storey inner courtyard house the statues and busts of famous writers, artists and scholars. The middle of the courtyard is dominated by the bronze statue of *Napoleon as a Victorious Hero*, which dates from 1809 and is the work of Antonio Canova. A monumental staircase leads up to the upper colonnade and the entrance to the gallery.

Star Attraction
● **Pinacoteca di Brera**

THE COLLECTION

The foundations for this art collection were laid at the end of the 18th and beginning of the 19th century, when it was originally intended to be a didactic collection for the Academy of Fine Arts. At the express wishes of Napoleon, his stepson Eugène Beauharnais had the art gallery opened to the public in 1809. With the oppression of various religious orders and their churches brought about by secularisation, numerous religious works of art were acquired by the state and added to the collection.

During the course of the 19th and 20th centuries the collection has expanded considerably through purchases and donations, and it is still growing. It was further endowed with important works of contemporary art by the donations of the Jesi

Palazzo Cusani
At Via Brera 15 is the imposing Palazzo Cusani (closed to the public). Originally constructed in the 17th century, the palace was extended in 1719 by the architect Ruggeri in the ornate style of the high baroque. The garden frontage, which can be seen from the Via del Carmine, is by Piermarini in a transitional style between baroque and neoclassicism. Nowadays the palace is used as a centre for musical documentation and a multimedia archive.

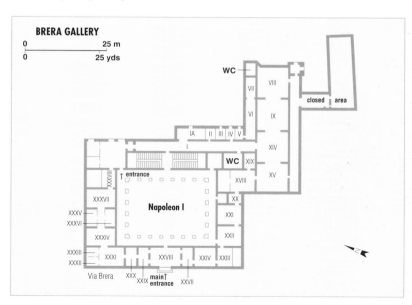

BRERA GALLERY

0 — 25 m
0 — 25 yds

WC

VII   VIII

closed   area

VI   IX

IA II III IV V

I   XIV

WC   XIX

entrance   XVIII   XV

XXXIX   XX

XXXVII   Napoleon I

XXXV   XXI

XXXVI

XXXIV   XXII

XXXIII   XXXI   XXVIII   XXIV   XXIII

XXXII

Via Brera   XXX   main entrance   XXVII
            XXIX

Map on page 37

family. The Brera has around 2,500 works in its possession, principally by Italian masters of the 14th to 20th centuries, of which around 560 exhibits are on display in more than 30 rooms.

Since the mid-1970s a programme of renovation and reorganisation has been underway to ensure that the gallery conforms to the changing needs of visitors, such as educational activities and changing exhibitions.

ROOMS 1 TO 4

The hall (Room 1) contains the impressive Jesi modern art collection, the emphasis of which is on Italian art from the first half of the 20th century. The collection includes works by the most influential figures in Italian art from that period, such as Amedeo Modigliani, Umberto Boccioni, Carlo Carrà, Filippo de Pisis, Giorgio Morandi, Mario Sironi, Marino Marini and Medardo Rosso. There are also works by important European painters of the same period from outside of Italy, including Pablo Picasso, Pierre Bonnard and Georges Braque.

In Room 1a is a reconstruction of the chapel of Count Porro in Mocchirolo near Lentante, with the magnificent Gothic frescos (1365–70) by a Lombard master, possibly Pietra da Nova. The frecoes include: *Crucifixion*, *Christ and the Four*

Mario Marini
This artist (1901–80), who trained as a painter, went on to become one of the most important 20th-century Italian sculptors (his horse and rider sculptures are especially highly regarded). Despite training in Florence and Paris, he is closely linked with Milan, since much of his working life was spent here. Several of his pieces are on show in the Pinacoteca di Brera; others are on show in Milan's Museo Marini, founded by the artist himself in 1974.

Paesaggio Con Cathion by Mario Sironi (1920)

Evangelists, Count Porro with Members of his Family Offering the Virgin a Model of the Chapel, St Ambrose Enthroned Scourging Two Heretics, and the *Mystic Marriage of St Catherine.*

Rooms 2 to 4 showcase religious pictures from the 13th to 15th centuries, predominantly panel paintings and fragments of larger works that formed the altarpieces in the churches of the period. Painters represented include Giovanni Baronzio, Ambrogio Lorenzetti, Giovanni da Milano, Giovanni da Bologna, Nicolò di Pietro, Andrea di Bartolo, Stefano da Verona and Gentile da Fabriano.

ROOMS 5 TO 14

The next series of rooms cover Venetian art of the Renaissance period. Rooms 5 and 6 feature Venetian paintings of the 15th and 16th centuries, including, in Room 5, the *Praglia Polyptych* by Giovanni d'Alemagna and Antonio Vivarini, *Dead Christ with Angels* by Girolamo da Treviso the Elder and *St Mark* by Master Giorgio; in Room 6 are an important *Pietà* and two paintings of the *Virgin and Child* by Giovanni Bellini, an eerily foreshortened *Dead Christ* by Andrea Mantegna and the *Marriage of the Virgin* and *Presentation of the Virgin* by Vittore Carpaccio.

In Room 7 are Venetian portraits of the 16th century including Lorenzo Lotto's *Portrait of an Elderly Gentleman with Gloves* and *Laura da Pola*, Titian's *Portrait of Count Antonio Porcia* and works by Tintoretto.

More Venetian paintings are displayed in Room 8, all dating from the 15th century. Works include the huge *St Mark Preaching in Alexandria* by Gentile and Giovanni Bellini, one of the Brera's most famous paintings, and works by Bartolomeo Montagna (his *Virgin and Child Enthroned with St Andrew, St Monica, St Ursula and St Sigismund*), Francesco Morone, Giovanni Mansueti, Alvise Vivarini and others.

Rooms 9 to 13 are devoted to the greatest splendour of 16th-century Venetian painting and house some of the most stunning works in the collection.

Below: Brera sign
Bottom: Portrait of a Gentleman by Fra' Galgario

Map on page 37

Below: Madonna and Child
Bottom: St Sebastian

Important pieces on show include Titian's *St Jerome in Penitence*, Veronese's *Last Supper* and *Baptism and Temptation of Christ*, Tintoretto's *Pietà* and *Finding of the Body of St Mark*, plus a *Pietà* by Lorenzo Lotto.

In Room 14 are Venetian paintings of the 16th century including Moretto da Brescia's *Virgin and Child* and Giovanni Battista Moroni's *Virgin and Child with St Catherine, St Francis and Donor*.

ROOMS 15 TO 19

The gallery focuses, in Room 15, on Lombard paintings and frescoes of the 15th and 16th centuries, including Bramantino's *Virgin and Child and a Two Angels* and *Crucifixion*, and Vincenzo Foppa's Polyptych *Santa Maria delle Grazie*.

The Pinacoteca's numbering system now becomes confused, and the next room you reach is number 18; here, you'll see Lombard paintings of the 16th century, including Altobello Melone's *Portrait of Alda Gambara*, Callisto Piazza's *Baptism of Christ* and a series of four paintings by Vincenzo Campi, considered to be the forerunners of the still life genre in Italy.

Room 19 shows Lombard religious paintings and portraits of the 15th and 16th centuries, including Bergognone's *Virgin and Child, St Catherine of Siena and a Carthusian Monk*, Andrea Solario's *Portrait of a Young Man* and *Virgin and Child with St Joseph and St Simeon*, and Bernardino Luini's *Madonna of the Rose Garden*.

ROOMS 20 TO 23

In Room 20 are 15th-century paintings from Ferrara and Emilia Romagna, including Francesco del Cossa's *St John the Baptist* and *St Peter*, Cosmè Tura's dramatic *Crucifixion* and Lorenzo Costa's *Adoration of the Magi*. In Room 21 are 15th-century polyptychs from the Marches, including *St Peter* by Fra Carnevale (Maestro delle Tavole Barberini), Girolamo di Giovanni's *Gualdo Tadino* and Carlo Crivelli's lavish *Coronation of the Virgin*.

Continue on to Rooms 22 and 23 to see 15th-
and 16th-century paintings from Ferrara and
Emilia Romagna. In Room 22 highlights include
Marco Palmezzano's *Virgin and Child with
Saints*, Lodovico Mazzolino's *Raising of Lazarus*
and Dosso Dossi's *St Sebastian*; in Room 23 look
for Correggio's *Nativity* and *Adoration of the Magi*.

Star Attraction
● **Pinacoteca di Brera**

ROOMS 24 TO 29

Rooms 24 to 26 house some of the finest works
in the Brera, including *Madonna with Child,
Angels, Saints and Federico da Montefeltro* by
Piero della Francesca (an altarpiece taken from
the church of San Bernardino in Urbino), a *Marriage of the Virgin* by Raphael and *Christ at the
Column* by Donato Bramante.

Painting from central Italy from the 15th and
16th centuries are on show in Room 27, including *Disputation over the Immaculate Conception*
by Girolamo Genga and *The Virgin Annunciate
with St John the Baptist and St Sebastian* by Tim-
oteo Viti. Room 28 covers central Italian painting from the 17th century, including Ludovico
Carracci's *Christ and the Samaritan Woman* and
The Sermon of St Anthony, and Guido Reni's *St
Peter and St Paul*.

Continue into Room 29 where you can see
work by Caravaggio (1570– 1610) and his pupils.

Brera painting

Map on page 37

Below: Francesco Hayez's The Kiss
Bottom: Brera courtyard

Of note are the magnificent *Supper at Emmaus* by Caravaggio, *Christ and the Samaritan Woman* by Battistello Caracciolo, and *The Martyrs Valerian, Tiburtius and Cecilia* by Orazio Gentileschi.

In Room 30 are Lombard painting from the 17th century, including *The Mystic Marriage of St Catherine* by Giulio Cesare Procaccini and *Virgin of the Rosary* by Cerano.

ROOMS 31 TO 38

The next section of the Pinacoteca provides a change from the Lombard and Venetian art that dominates the gallery. In Room 31 are Flemish and Italian paintings of the 17th century, including works by Rubens, Van Dyck, Jacob Jordaens and Pietro da Cortona. These works are followed by Flemish and Dutch paintings of the 16th century (Room 32) and, in Room 33, painting from the 17th century, including works by Jan de Beer, Rubens, Brueghel the Elder and Van Dyck.

Religious paintings of the 18th century, including works by Tiepolo, Subleyras and Bottan are displayed in Room 34, while Room 35 houses 18th-century Venetian paintings, with pieces by Piazzetta, Canaletto *(The Bacino di San Marco from the Point of the Dogana)* and Bellotto. Room 36 shows Italian 18th-century genre painting and portraiture, including works by Crespi and Ceruti.

The final Rooms, 37 and 38, house Italian 19th-century painting, including Francesco Hayez's important sentimental work, *The Kiss*. Exit via Giuseppe Pelizza da Volpedo's *Fourth Estate*.

Star Attraction
● Pinacoteca di Brera

SANTA MARIA DEL CARMINE

After visiting the Palazzo di Brera, cross Via Brera and walk down Via del Carmine. On your right is the church of **Santa Maria del Carmine** ㉚ (Mon–Fri 7.15–11.30am and 3.30–7pm, Sat and Sun till 7.30pm). This church, which belongs to the Carmelite monastery, was begun in 1339 according to the plans of Bernardo da Venezia, but then suddenly collapsed in 1446. It was subsequently rebuilt in late-Gothic style under the direction of Pietro Solaris. After undergoing several major alterations down the centuries, the façade was converted into a Lombard Gothic fantasy style by Maciachini in 1879. Among the features particularly worth seeing on the inside is the splendid baroque chapel (1616–76) in the right transept, designed by Giovanni Quadrio. It was embellished with valuable, partly painted marble decorations by Camillo Procaccini. In the first chapel on the left there is a *Madonna with Child and Saints* (17th century) by Procaccini, while the fourth chapel on the left contains an early work by Bernardino Luini on the same theme (late 15th century). In the adjoining cloister there are fragments of Roman reliefs, medieval capitals and various sculptures by Campione masters.

Francesco Hayez
Born in 1791, in Venice, Hayez lived in Rome and Florence before settling, in 1822, in Milan. He was appointed Professor of Art at the Brera in 1850 and in 1860 was made Director. His most notable work, *The Kiss*, is now housed in the museum and is in the sentimental style of painting influenced by Romantic artists such as Delacroix.

Statue in front of Santa Maria del Carmine

SAN SIMPLICIANO

Now turn onto Via Mercato Vetero and walk north (to your right). At the point where the road changes into Corso Garibaldi, turn right into Via Pontaccio, which then leads onto a right turn down Via San Simpliciano. Soon Piazza Crociate comes into view, with its ancient church of **San Simpliciano** ㉑ (Mon–Fri 7am–noon and 3–7pm, Sat and Sun 8am–noon and 4–7pm), one of the most beautiful churches in Milan.

Map on page 37

Battle stations

Legend has it that on 29 May 1176, the day of the Battle of Legnano between the Lombard League and Barbarossa, three white doves flew out of the room in San Simpliciano where the relics of three martyrs (Martirio, Sisinio and Alessandro) were kept. They landed on the flagpoles and spured the communes on to victory. In commemoration, balloons are released on 29 May every year in the square in front of the church.

San Simpliciano was probably founded by St Ambrose during the 4th century on the site of an ancient Roman cemetery and completed by Ambrose's successor, St Simplician, who lies buried here. Traces of the Early Christian structure can still be clearly seen on the side walls of the three-aisled interior. Despite alterations over the centuries, the church has retained its Romanesque appearance; the campanile, however, was considerably reduced in height at the request of the Spanish government, since it used to be higher than the nearby Castello Sforzesco, which lay within firing distance. Concerts are often held here and in the nearby church of San Marco *(see opposite)*.

HIGHLIGHTS

Early highlights inside the church include the altar slab (beneath the neoclassical *baldacchino*), a 5th- or 6th-century marble parapet. Also of note are the *Wise and Foolish Virgins* from the Gospel of St Matthew, sculpted on the capitals of the 12th-century central portal in the façade. In the apse, the large ★ *Coronation of the Virgin* **fresco** (*circa* 1515), depicting God the Father embracing the Virgin and Jesus, is an important example of the work of Ambrogio da Fossano (Bergognone), while the statues of the saints on the organ loft are by Aurelio Luini, son of the

Stained glass, San Simpliciano

great Bernardino. On the left, just opposite the sacristy, is the remarkable 17th-century altarpiece *Marriage of the Virgin*, by Procaccini. The much-later painted glass on the inner wall of the façade (1927) is based on designs by Aldo Carpi and was executed by Trevarotto; it depicts episodes from the battle of Legnano.

CLOISTERS

To visit San Simpliciano's cloisters, contact the Facoltà Teologica Interregionale dell'Italia Settentrionale (the porter's lodge is at house No 6; Tues–Fri 9am–1pm and 2–6pm, Mon by appointment). The cloisers are two-fold: first, you'll pass a Renaissance cloister dating from 1449, followed by the Chiostro delle Due Colonne, a two-storey structure with double columns, built during the 16th century.

SAN MARCO

Next stop is **San Marco** ㉒ (Mon–Sat 7am–noon, 4–7pm, Sun 7am–1pm). With a length of 95m (315ft), this is Milan's second largest church after the Duomo. It is said that it was founded in 1254 by Lanfranco da Settala, who was later to become master of the Augustinian Order. Alterations were made in the 14th century and again in the 17th.

After the deconsecration of the patricians' cemetery that had been added to the church in the 15th century, between the 16th and 19th century nine chapels housing family tombs were built along the right-hand side of the building. The top of the transept has retained its 13th-century appearance, and the campanile dates from the 14th century.

The brick façade was restored in 1871 by Maciachini in the Lombard Gothic style; the middle portal with its pointed arch and architrave decorated with scenes from the life of Christ, symbols of the Evangelists and two saints, is part of the structure that originally stood on the site. Three niches above the portal contain statues of saints Mark, Ambrose and Augustine.

Below: San Simpliciano
Bottom: San Marco

Map on page 37

Prada
Established in Milan in 1913 by Mario Prada, the family firm of Fratelli Prada started by crafting luxury leather goods for the rich and famous. Mario's grand-daugther, Miuccia, inherited the business in 1978. Although unschooled in fashion design – she has a PhD in political science – Miuccia has taken the firm from strength to strength. She has expanded into mens- and womenswear, producing universally acclaimed collections dominated by clean, almost stark, lines and hip, yet subtle, decoration. She introduced a more affordable line under her nickname, Miu Miu, opening the market for Prada goods even further.

Statue of St Francis in Piazza Sant'Angelo

The baroque interior dates from 1694. The family chapels in the right-hand side-aisle contain some fine paintings, and the right transept, with all its tomb inscriptions and monuments, is of particular interest – especially the 13th-century sarcophagus of St Lanfranco da Settala, a work by Giovanni di Balduccio.

To the right of the main altar in the apse is the large 17th-century painting *Dispute Between saints Ambrose and Augustine* by Camillo Procaccini, and on the left-hand side is the *Baptism of St Augustine* (1618) by Cerano. On the left-hand side of the left transept is the Cappella della Pietà with its *Entombment of Christ* altarpiece (a copy in the style of Caravaggio).

MUSEO DEL RISORGIMENTO

Now head back to Via Fiori Oscuri and cross straight over into Via Borgonuovo. At No 23, is the **Museo del Risorgimento** ㉓ (Tues–Sun 9.30am–5.30pm). The museum, which is housed in the Palazzo de Marchi (erected in 1775 to designs by Piermarini), contains objects from the struggles of the Italian Unity Movement and memorabilia of Napoleon I (including the royal insignia and the robe he wore for his coronation as King of Italy) as well as exhibits from both world wars.

SANT'ANGELO

Retrace your steps to Via Fiori Oscuri but turn right where Fiori Oscuri becomes Via dell' Annunciata. Relatively soon, turn left up Corso Porta Nuova and walk as far as Piazza Sant'Angelo, and the church of **Sant'Angelo** ㉔ (Sun–Fri 6.30am– 8pm). This Franciscan church was built in the Late Renaissance style by Domenico Giunti in 1552. The interior is a study in monastic austerity and simplicity; hardly surprising since the adjacent monastery has been the seat of the Franciscan Order, whose monks embrace a life of poverty, since 1730.

Next to the church is the entrance to the so-called *Angelicum*, an exhibition centre. In Piazza Sant'Angelo is the Fountain of St Francis (1927, by Giannino Castiglioni), a real favourite with the Milanese: the rather effete-looking saint is shown speaking to the pigeons on the edge of the fountain, while fish splash inside it.

Brera shopping highlights

SHOPPING HEAVEN

Once you've sated your yearning for culture by visiting the galleries and churches of the Brera, it may be time to wind down and indulge yourself with some actual or window-shopping in the district's ultra-stylish boutiques. On Via Solferino, you'll find one-off clothes stores (mostly for women) and a scattering of cool shoe shops, showcasing the designer heels for which Milan is famed; purchasing such footwear and actually managing to tread the city's cobbled streets in them are two different matters, however.

The cobbled Via Fiori Chiari has some designer boutiques and small commercial art galleries, but these sit side by side with bars and cafés, where you can relax for a while and soak up the local atmosphere. On summer evenings, this street comes alive as the Milanese undertake their *passeggiata*, or evening stroll, and street-vendors try their hardest to sell fake Louis Vuitton and Prada bags. Note that on the third Saturday of the month, a lively antiques market spills on to Via Fiori Chiari.

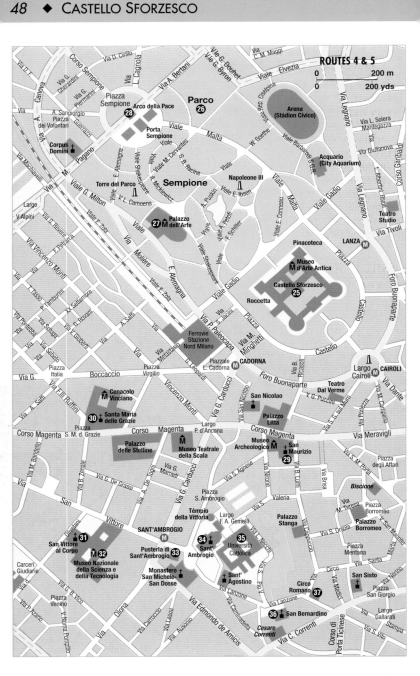

4: Castello Sforzesco

This route covers Milan's Castello Sforzesco – a sprawling fortress built by the Viscontis in the 14th century and expanded by the Sforza dynasty from the mid-15th century. The castle is home to several museums, including an ancient arts museum, a gallery and one of Europe's best museums of musical instruments.

It's certainly worth a visit, whether for a meander through the attractive grounds, or a more lengthy visit to fully explore the collection. The route also takes you to Parco Sempione, the vast park located just behind the castle.

CASTLE HISTORY

The ★★★ **Castello Sforzesco** ㉕ (grounds open daily 8am–8pm; museums open Tues–Sun 9.30am–5.30pm) was originally known as the Castello di Porta Giovia, after a small gate in the medieval city wall that was later built into the castle walls. The western section, the Rocchetta, was laid out as a fortress in 1368 by Galeazzo II Visconti; it was partly destroyed by the people of Milan during the riots that followed the death of the last Visconti in 1447.

It was then rebuilt by Francesco Sforza from 1450. Sforza extended the original castle building, adding the Corte Ducale and the Cortile delle Milizie. Francesco's son Galeazzo Maria and his widow Bona of Savoy completed the extension to the castle between 1466 and 1477.

IL MORO AND THE GOLDEN AGE

During the late 15th century Ludovico il Moro commissioned artists including Leonardo da Vinci and Bramante to work on the Castello, which by then was already one of the greatest Italian castles of the period, with accommodation for 800 courtiers and servants. However, in 1499 Ludovico was captured by the French and both castle and court fell into decline; matters culminated with Napoleon I razing its fortifications.

Map opposite

Star Attraction
● Castello Sforzesco

Fountain in front of the Castello Sforzesco

Maps on page 48 & below

As the 19th century drew to a close, it looked likely that the castle would be demolished, but in 1893, thanks mainly to the campaigning efforts of architect Luca Beltrami, the city of Milan had the castle restored in 15th-century style. Further renovation was necessary after World War II.

CORTILE DELLE MILIZIE

The Cortile delle Milizie (also known as the Piazza d'Armi) is reached through the Torre dell'Orologio clock tower *(see box, left)*. Across to the left is the **Cortile della Rocchetta**, to which the dukes would retire whenever danger threatened. Almost at the centre of the courtyard façade is the huge 35-m (120-ft) high **Tower of Bona of Savoy**, erected in 1477.

Beyond the Cortile delle Milizie we now pass through a square gate, built on the site of the

Clock tower

At the centre of the castle's Piazza Castello façade is the 70-m (250-ft) high quadrilateral clock tower, the Torre dell'Orologio (also known as Torre Umberto I or Torre di Filarete). This tapering tower (1905) is a copy of the gate added by Filarete in the 15th century. A bas-relief above the portal shows Umberto I on horseback; above that is a statue of Milan's patron saint, Ambrose, flanked by six Sforza family ducal coats-of-arms.

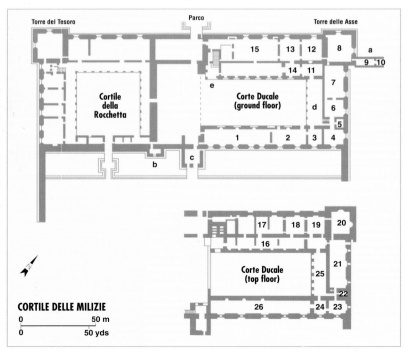

Torre del Tesoro   Parco   Torre delle Asse

Cortile della Rocchetta

Corte Ducale (ground floor)

15   13   12   8   a
9   10
14   11
7
e
d   6
5
1   2   3   4

c
b

Corte Ducale (top floor)

17   18   19   20
16
21
25
22
26   24   23

CORTILE DELLE MILIZIE

0 ——————— 50 m
0 ——————— 50 yds

former Porta Giovia and bearing the Sforza arms and a *Crucifixion* fresco (*circa* 1470) by an anonymous Lombard artist. This leads to the Ducal Courtyard, the ducal residence proper.

CIVICI MUSEI DEL CASTELLO

Located on the ground floor of the Ducal Courtyard is the entrance to the ★ **Civici Musei del Castello** (Sforza Castle Art Galleries; Tues–Sun 9.30am–5.30pm). Some 26 halls are dedicated to this extensive collection of works, from mummies to musical instruments to Michelangelo's masterpieces. The following aims to pick out the highlights. Note that the museums are well labelled in English.

The visit begins with the **Raccolte D'Arte Antica** (Museum of Ancient Art).

ROOMS 1 TO 4

The first four rooms on the ground floor house sculpture from the early Christian to Gothic periods. In Room 1 are fragments of mosaic pavements, tomb frescoes and the remains of buildings, capitals and sarcophagi from the 4th to 9th centuries. Room 2 displays Romanesque art, notably a large 14th-century equestrian statue that was the funeral monument of Bernabò Visconti by Bonino da Campione. In Room 3 is the 15th-century ceiling fresco of the Resurrection by an unknown artist and 14th-century sculpture including votive statues of the Virgin that once adorned the city's former gates.

On the ceiling of Room 4, a coat-of-arms depicts the emblems of Philip II of Spain and his wife Mary Tudor (1555). Also on show here are several fragments by Giovanni di Balduccio from the 14th-century church façade of Santa Maria di Brera.

ROOMS 5 TO 10

More 14th-century sculpture is on show in Room 5, while Room 6 documents Milanese history. Note, in Room 6, the bas-reliefs of the former Porta

Below: outer walls of the Castello Sforzesco
Bottom: stained glass showing the Sforza coat-of-arms

Maps
on pages
48 & 50

👁 **Elephant fresco**
Inside the Ducal Courtyard is an open-air hall and portico commissioned by Galeazzo Maria Sforza in the late 15th century. The portico is known as the **Portico dell'Elefante** after a fresco by Benedetto Ferrini decorating the walls; the fresco portrays an elephant. There were originally other animals, including lions, in the fresco but nowadays there are only faint reminders of these – you can still see the lion's hind paws if you look carefully.

Painting from the Castello Sforzesco's collection

Romana; these date from the 12th century and depict both the expulsion of the Arians by St Ambrose and the triumphal return of the Milanese after the Battle of Legnano against Barbarossa.

Lombard and Flemish tapestries from the 17th century decorate the walls of Room 7, while in the middle of the hall is the banner of Milan (1566, by Giuseppe Meda) with embroidered scenes from the life of St Ambrose.

Room 8 – also known as the Sala delle Asse because of its former 15th-century panelling – is furnished with beautiful frescoes by Leonardo da Vinci. The frescoes, which were heavily restored in 1902, depict a mock balcony with trees (and the arms of Lodovico il Moro).

The next hall (Room 9, known as the Saletta Negra) was often used by Lodovico il Moro for meditation and contemplation after the death of his wife, Beatrice d'Este; it was once decorated by Leonardo, although all that now remains of his work is a panel bearing the inscription: 'Everything that Mortals Consider as Happy is Finally Sad.' On the walls are medallion portraits of the Sforza family, which date from the early 16th century and are by Bernardino Luini. In Room 10 there are further portraits of the Sforza by Luini.

ROOMS 11 TO 13

The Sala dei Ducali (Room 11) bears the arms of the Sforza dynasty and the initials of Galeazzo Maria (GZ), above which Lodovico il Moro had his own placed (LU). The hall contains several late-Gothic sculptures, including a bas-relief featuring allegorical scenes.

The Cappella Ducale (Duke's Chapel, Room 12) was built between 1472 and 1473 by Benedetto Ferrini, who received the commission from Galeazzo Maria. The Resurrection fresco on the ceiling and the saints on the walls are by Stefano de Fedeli and his pupils. In the middle of the room is a 15th-century *Madonna in Prayer,* attributed to Pietro Solari.

The next room, the Sala delle Colombine (Hall of the Doves, Room 13) is named after its fresco depicting doves, commissioned by Bona of Savoy. Also on show here are several important 15th-century Lombard sculptures and two 16th-century angels by Amadeo.

Star Attraction
● **Michelangelo's**
Pietà Rondanini

ROOMS 14 TO 15

Room 14, known as the Sala Verde (it was once green in colour) contains the castle's weapon collection and several magnificent Renaissance portals, including one belonging to the Medici Bank in Milan (1455), by Michelozzo.

Below: Pietà Rondanini
Bottom: Resurrection fresco, Castello ceiling

The Sala degli Scarlioni (Room 15) is named after the zigzag decoration in the Sforza colours that was used to decorate the walls. The hall consists of two rooms, which house two jewels in the castle's crown. In the first room is the fine funerary statue of French leader Gaston de Foix (1525), who died in Milan in 1512. The work is by Agostino Busti, also known as il Bambaia, and is a fine example of the Lombard classical style of the early 16th century. The second room, which is reached via a broad staircase, contains the most notable artwork in the castle's collection, the ★★ *Pietà Rondanini*; this sculpture was Michelangelo's last work and is named after its original location in Palazzo Rondanini. The artist is believed to have been working on it only a few days before his death in 1564 and it remains unfinished.

Below and bottom: paintings
from the Pinacoteca

ROOMS 16–19

To reach the next set of rooms, on the first floor of the Ducal Courtyard, take the wooden walkway across the Cortile della Fontana (Fountain Courtyard); an old stairway (Scala Cavallina) on the right then leads to the upper floors.

The first four halls showcase items from the Castello's vast furniture collection, of which there are around 600 pieces in total. Most of the furniture on show is domestic and from Northern Italy. Hall 17 also contains a fresco cycle from Castello Roccabianco, near Parma, depicting Griseldi's story from Boccaccio's *Decameron*.

PINACOTECA

The remainder of the halls are devoted to the ★★ **Pinacoteca** (Picture Gallery), which gives an overview of Italian painting from the 14th to 18th centuries. The majority of work on show is from the Lombard School.

The Sala Dorata (Room 20) contains late-Gothic and early-Renaissance works by various schools, including a delicate *Madonna in Humility* by Filippo Lippi; an important *Madonna and Child* by Giovanni Bellini; the spectacular *Virgin Mary and Child with Saints and Angels in Glory* by Andrea Mantegna and various works by Lorenzo Veneziano and Carlo Crivelli.

Room 21 is dedicated to 16th-century paintings, with highlights including three moving portraits of the Virgin with child (*Madonna con Bambino*), by Bellini, Cesare da Sesto and Correggio. The tiny room next door (22) contains Giulio Cesare Procaccini's dark *Constantine Receiving Instruments of Torture*.

Rooms 23 and 24 contain works by the leading exponents of Lombard Mannerism, including Bernadino Campi, Giuseppe Arcimboldi and Cesare Procaccini (note his noble *Martyrdom of St Sebastian*).

The final hall (26) shows 17th- and 18th-century masters, including paintings by Magnasco (*The Verziere Market*), Bernardo Strozzi (*Berenice*), and Cerano (*The Archangel Michael*).

ROCHETTA MUSEUMS

Back at the main entrance to the Ducal Court-yard is a staircase that leads to the first and second floors of the **Rocchetta**, where two further museums are housed. In the same part of the castle (the first floor) is the Sala della Balla (usually closed since it is used for civic receptions), home to the *Trivulzio* tapestries; created in 1503 according to designs by Bramantino, the tapestries show 12 allegories of the months. They are named after the Milanese nobleman who commissioned them.

The ★★ **Museo degli Strumenti Musicali** (Museum of Musical Instruments), on the first floor of the Rocchetta, contains around 650 exhibits and is the most comprehensive museum of its kind in Europe. Highlights include violins by master-makers Gasparo da Salò and Guarneri, Mango Longo's ten-string guitar, Johannes Maria Anciuti's oboe (1722) and a rare glass harmonica, which had once belonged to Pietro Verri.

On the second floor of the Rocchetta is the **Civiche Raccolte d'Arte Applicata** (Applied Arts Museum), which chronologically showcases works in a large range of media, from the Middle Ages to the 19th century. The collection includes wrought iron (Room 28), ceramics (Rooms 29 and 30), European porcelain (Room 31), liturgical items and scientific instruments (Room 32) and leatherware (Room 35).

Star Attraction
● Pinacoteca
● Museo degli Strumenti Musicali

Early collections
Prehistoric and Egyptian collections are on show in the basement of the castle, below the Cortile della Rocchetta. The Prehistoric Collection includes archaeological finds from Palaeolithic times to the Iron Age; sections of lake dwellings from the Lagozza di Besnate are of special note, as are the remains of the Golasecca culture (Iron Age) and various Celtic finds. The small Egyptian Collection includes sarcophagi, mummies, statues, jewels and other burial items.

Castello Sforzesco coat-of-arms

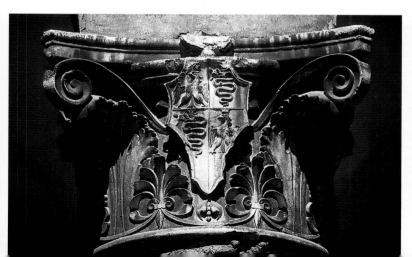

Maps
on pages
48 & 50

Cimitero Monumentale
North of Parco Sempione id
Milan's cemetery, Cimitero
Monumentale (Apr–Sep 8.30am–
5.15pm; Oct–Mar 8.30am– 4.30pm;
closed Mon). The burial ground, which
covers approximately 20 hectares
(50 acres), was designed in the
Lombard Gothic style by Carlo Maciachini and opened in 1860; it has
often been described as a sculpture
museum. At the centre of the cemetery façade is a large building known
as the Famedio (Temple of Honour),
which is dedicated to several famous
Milanese; those buried in the cemetery include the poet Alessandro Manzoni and the writer Carlo Cattaneo,
who initiated the Cinque Giornate
uprising of 1848.

Monument to Bianchini,
Cimitero Monumentale

CASTLE TREASURY

The courtyard of the Rocchetta is flanked on three sides by arcaded walkways dating from the late 15th century. The courtyard leads to the treasury *(tesoro),* where the ducal treasure was once housed. There is a remarkable 15th-century fresco here of the 100-eyed *Argus* by Bramante. Beneath it a small door leads to a room where the most valuable items in the collection were kept.

PARCO SEMPIONE

Leave Castello Sforzesco by its northwest gate, the Porta del Barco; on the other side of the moat is ★★**Parco Sempione** ㉖ (open daily 6.30am–8pm, later in summer). This English-style park, measuring 47 hectares (116 acres) in size and featuring lawns, twisting paths, copses and a lake, was laid out in 1893 according to plans by Emilio Alemagna.

CITY AQUARIUM

On the right is the **Civico Acquario e Stazione Idrobiologico** (open daily 9.30am–5.30pm), the city aquarium, and, beyond it, the Arena, or Stadio Civico, which was modelled on the stadia of antiquity by Luigi Canonica and opened in the presence of Napoleon I in 1807. Originally built to host horse- and coach-races as well as mock naval battles, nowadays the arena is used for sports events as well as the occasional musical show, and can accommodate around 30,000 spectators. The longitudinal axis (238m/780ft) lies between the Porta Trionfale and the Porta delle Carceri, where the coaches and horses were formerly kept. The broadest part of the arena extends from the Pulvinare (Princes' Box) and the Porta Libitinaria, recalling the gravediggers of the Roman amphitheatres who had to drag dying gladiators out of similar gates.

PALAZZO DELL'ARTE

In the western part of the park is the **Palazzo dell'Arte** ㉗, built in 1933 and the permanent headquarters of the Milan Triennale (open Tues–Sun 10am–8pm, closed Mon). It stages important exhibitions organised by the Triennale, including architecture and design, town planning, decorative arts and fashion. Not far away is the 108-m (340-ft) high iron viewing tower known as the **Torre del Parco**. On the hill of Monte Tondo there is a monument to Napoleon III.

Star Attraction
● **Parco Sempione**

ARCO DELLA PACE

At the end of the park is the Piazzale Sempione, with its **Arco della Pace** 28 (Peace Arch). This Roman-style triumphal arch in honour of Napoleon Bonaparte was designed by Cagnola and begun in 1807. In 1826, the Austrian Emperor Francis I dedicated it to the memory of the 1815 Congress of Vienna as an Arch of Peace. Since 1859 the arch has stood as a reminder of the triumphal march into the city by the Piedmontese-French troops under Vittorio Emanuele II and Napoleon III. The neoclassical arch is 25m (82ft) high and 24m (80ft) wide. On the attic is a bronze statue with six horses representing peace (by Abbondio Sangiorgio) and four goddesses of victory on horseback (by Giovanni Putti). At the very top are allegorical depictions of the main rivers of Lombardy and Venetia: the Po, Ticino, Adige and Tagliamento.

Below and bottom: City Aquarium, Parco Sempione

Map on page 48

5: West of the Centre

Milan seems to have more than its fair share of churches, and this route takes you to several of the most important in the area west of the centre. The highlight of the tour is a visit to the refectory adjacent to the church of Santa Maria della Grazie, where you can see the jewel in Milan's artistic crown, Leonardo da Vinci's *Last Supper*. (You are strongly advised to book tickets for this at least three days in advance of your visit.)

Palazzo Litta

SAN MAURIZIO

Start the route in front of Stazione Cadorna, on Piazzale Cadorna. From here, take Via Carducci as far as Corso Magenta and turn left into the latter. On Corso Magenta, you'll pass the impressive **Palazzo Litta**, designed in 1648, by Richini, with a rococo façade added in 1763. A little further on is the church of **San Maurizio** ㉙ (open Mon–Fri 4–6pm, Sun 10.30–11.30am). Also known as the Chiesa del Monastero Maggiore, this building was once the monastery church of a powerful Benedictine convent. The present structure, designed by Bramantino, was erected between 1503 and 1519 by Giacomo Dolcebuono and Cristoforo Solari. The unpretentious façade dates from 1574–81, while the gable on top is a baroque addition.

INTERIOR

The interior of the church consists of a nave with a row of chapels on either side, and a series of dwarf galleries (*see page 26*) in the upper section. A high wall separates the front section of the church, which is reserved for the congregation, from the rear section (formerly reserved for the nuns).

The walls in both sections of the church and the partition wall are covered with frescoes. To the left and right of the entry portal are frescoes depicting two New Testament scenes: the *Return of the Prodigal Son* and *Expulsion of the Money-lenders from the Temple* (16th century) by Simone

Peterzano. There are further wall paintings in the second chapel on the left, as well as an *Entombment* (1555) by Callisto Piazza. The frescoes in the third chapel on the right date from 1530 and were the last works by Bernardino Luini; they portray scenes from the life of St Catherine of Alexandria. The frescoes on the partition wall (1522) are also by Luini. The *Adoration of the Magi* decorating the main altar is by Antonio Campi. In the fourth chapel on the left is the passageway leading to the nuns' choir; the choir stalls have been attributed to Dolcebuono.

On the other side of the partition are further Luini frescoes, featuring angels, saints and scenes from the Passion, including his version of the *Last Supper*, which is interesting to compare with the more famous fresco by Leonardo da Vinci *(see page 60)*.

UPPER CLOISTER

A small stairway behind the choir leads to the upper cloister, where some delightful statues of female saints in 26 medallions (1505–10, by Boltraffio) are on show. The towers beyond the apse are believed to be Roman; the square one probably belonged to the prison at the Circus Maximus, and the polygonal one was part of a defensive wall built in the reign of the Emperor Maximilian.

Museo Archeologico
To the right of the church of San Maurizio, at Corso Magenta 15, is the entrance to the former Monastero Maggiore (home to Milan's most influential group of nuns), which is now home to the **Civico Museo Archeologico** (Archaeology Museum; Tues–Sun 9am–5.30pm). Highlights include a 2nd-century portrait of Maximilian, the 4th-century gilded silver Parabiago platter and the magnificent glass Trivulzio cup (Coppa Trivulzio).

Luini fresco, San Maurizio

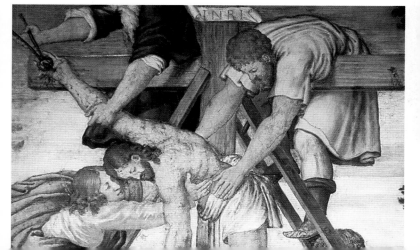

Map on page 48

SANTA MARIA DELLE GRAZIE

Now take the Corso Magenta in a westerly direction, passing the Casa Atellani at Nos 65 and 67; both buildings are typical 15th-century structures. On the opposite side of the street is the magnificent church of ★★ **Santa Maria delle Grazie** ③⓿ (open daily 7.30am–noon and 3–7pm) constructed in a Gothic-Renaissance transitional style between 1465 and 1490 by Guiniforte Solari. A new apse and cupola were added soon afterwards by Bramante, who received the commission from Ludovico il Moro. Bramante also constructed the magnificent marble portal in the façade.

Below and bottom: views of Santa Maria delle Grazie

The three-aisled interior (partly under restoration) has 15th-century fresco decoration in its groined vault, and the copestones on the ribs are decorated with reliefs of saints. On the pilasters in the side-aisles and in the lunettes of the nave there are several pictures of beatified Dominicans (15th century, by Butinone). The sacristy and little cloister are by Bramante, while the Great Cloister is after Solari.

The Last Supper

Most visitors make a pilgrimage to the church to see Leonardo da Vinci's ★★★ *Last Supper* (*Il Cenacolo*; Tues–Fri 8.15am–6.45pm, Sat 8.15am– 10.15pm, Sun 8.15am–6.45pm; it is

strongly advisable to book at least three days in advance, as tickets are usually sold out if you arrive without a reservation; booking on tel: 02-89421146). Commissioned from Leonardo by Ludovico il Moro and painted between 1495 and 1497, the fresco – which is 9m (30ft) long and 4.5m (14ft) high – covers the entire rear wall of the Cenacolo Vinciano, the former refectory of the Dominican Monastery that stands adjacent to Santa Maria delle Grazie.

Leonardo did not use traditional fresco painting techniques on the *Last Supper*, employing instead his own new technique of using tempera on a base mixed by himself on the stone wall. This procedure proved unsuccessful: the base began to loosen from the wall, and inadequate restoration work from the 17th to the 19th centuries only aggravated the situation. The rear of the wall was heated in 1908, but this made no noticeable difference. In 1943 the refectory was destroyed in a bombing raid, but, incredibly, the *Last Supper* remained unscathed. The most recent restoration on the work was finally completed in 1999, after 20 years.

Although this recent restoration has been heavily criticised for being somewhat lacklustre, it is generally considered to be very true to the original. The work has greatly improved the amount of detail visible on the fresco, converting what in patches were blurs of colour into detailed character studies. The masterpiece portrays the moment when Jesus tells his disciples, 'One of you shall betray me', and the power of this painting derives from the striking contrast in the attitudes of the 12 disciples to Christ; they are agitated, while Christ sits in quiet resignation. Leonardo has used facial features, hands and bodily position to express the reaction of each disciple to Christ's revelation.

Christ is portrayed in the process of speaking, gesturing with his right hand to the wine he is about to pour and with his left hand to the bread he is about to break. Judas Iscariot, third from Christ's right hand, clutches a bag of money. John, on Christ's right, recoils in disbelief at the thought

Star Attractions
- Santa Maria delle Grazie
- Leonardo's Last Supper

Also on show
Adorning the wall opposite The *Last Supper* is a fresco of the Crucifixion, executed in 1495 by Donato da Montorfano. The fresco contains scarcely discernable figures, added by Leonardo da Vinci, of Ludovico Sforza (founder and benefactor of Santa Maria delle Grazie) and two of his children.

Thirteenth-century fresco, Santa Maria delle Grazie

Maps
on pages
48 & 64

that he would betray his master. Peter, next to John, is gripping a knife that he will use later in the garden of Gethsemane to attack the servant of the high priest. Behind Philip, on Christ's left, is Thomas; he is pointing his finger upwards in a gesture that was used by Renaissance monks when in the Refectory (and subject to a vow of silence) to signify God.

At the end of the visit, there's a small shop where you can buy cards, gifts and souvenirs relating to the painting.

SAN VITTORE AL CORPO

Now leave the Refectory and head for Via Zenale; turn left down Via San Vittore to reach **San Vittore al Corpo** ❸ (open Mon–Sat 7.30am–noon and 3.30–7pm, Sun 8am–1pm). The church was constructed in its present form by Galeazzo Alessi in 1560. The interior contains 17th-century stucco work and frescoes, and some fine 16th-century choir stalls.

Next door, at No 21, is the former monastery of San Vittore; today it houses the **Museo Nazionale della Scienza e della Tecnologia 'Leonardo da Vinci'** ❷ (open Tues–Fri 9.30am–4.50pm, Sat and Sun 9.30am–6.30pm), Milan's science and technology museum. Among the collections documenting the history of technology

 Identifying the apostles
The figures depicted in the *Last Supper* are, from left to right, as follows:
1. Bartholomew
2. James the Lesser
3. Andrew
4. Judas Iscariot
5. Peter
6. John
7. Jesus Christ
8. Thomas
9. James the Elder
10. Philip
11. Matthew
12. Thaddeus
13. Simon

Leonardo's Last Supper

are Leonardo's actual ★★ **models**, which cast light on his far-advanced studies of fortifications, submarines and aviation devices.

SANT'AMBROGIO

The **Pusterla di Sant'Ambrogio** ㉝ is a 1939 copy of a sally-port that was built into the city wall in 1167; it was later used as a prison and today contains the **Museo della Pusterla di Sant'Ambrogio** (open daily 10am–7.30pm), showcasing weapons and torture instruments from the Middle Ages to the early 19th century. The figures dating from 1360 above the arches depict saints Ambrose, Gervase and Protasius.

Directly opposite is the basilica of ★★ **Sant' Ambrogio** ㉞ (daily 7am–noon and 2–7pm), which was built by Milan's patron saint, Ambrose, between 379 and 387 to house the relics of the martyrs Gervase and Protasius that were formerly buried in a cemetery on the same spot. Ambrose was buried here in 387 (his tomb is in the crypt). Altered in the 9th and 12th centuries, the basilica is the epitome of the Lombard Romanesque style.

THE ATRIUM AND FAÇADE

The basilica's rectangular atrium [**A**] *(see plan on next page)* dates back to 1150 and is surrounded by large arcades. The capitals on the columns are decorated with symbolic animals, acanthus leaves, centaurs and other mythological creatures. Below the arcades is a lapidarium containing Roman and Romanesque capitals, tombstones, and pagan and Early Christian inscriptions; there are also the remains of some 12th- and 13th-century frescoes on the walls.

To the left and right of the atrium are two towers: to the right is the 9th-century Campanile dei Monaci [**B**] (Monks' Tower), while to left is the Campanile dei Canonici [**C**] (Canons' Tower). The latter was erected between 1128 and 1144 in order to end a dispute about church bells between the canons and the Benedictine monks from the neighbouring monastery.

Star Attraction
● **Leonardo models**
● **Sant'Ambrogio**

Below and bottom: the Museo Nazionale della Scienza e della Tecnologia

Maps on
page 48
& below

The basilica's façade [**D**] consists of two super-imposed loggias, the upper one of which has five arcades. The lower hall has three portals, while the central one is framed by narrow columns and Romanesque decoration. The doors, which are beautifully carved in cypress wood and date from the 4th to 9th centuries, underwent extensive restoration during the 18th century. The great bronze door-knockers are Lombard and date from the 8th and 9th centuries, and the side portals with their massive architraves show likenesses of animals. On the left of the main portal is the marble tomb of the humanist Pier Candido Decembrio, sculpted in 1447 by Tomaso Cazzaniga.

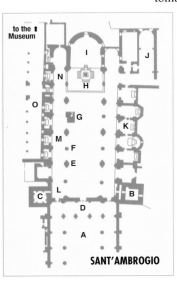

to the ↑
Museum

SANT'AMBROGIO

THE MAIN NAVE

Advance through the façade and, ahead and to the left, you'll see three early 13th-century frescoes on the piers [**E**]. The frescoes are of *St Ambrose*, the *Virgin and Child* and *The Founder Bonamico Taverna*. Tenth-century Byzantine columns [**F**] featuring bronze serpents – which, according to legend, belonged to Moses – are located just in front of the frescoes.

The basilica's pulpit [**G**] *(ambo)* was originally built in the 11th century, and rebuilt after it collapsed in 1201. Beneath it is a 4th-century sarcophagus, which is said to contain the remains of Stilicho (a general in the army of Emperor Theodosius the Great) and his wife Serena. The central relief on the sarcophagus depicts *Christ and the Scholars*; to the right of it are *Elijah and his Chariot of Fire* and *Noah and Moses*, while on the back is *Christ and the Apostles*, and to the left, *The Sacrifice of Abraham*.

THE ALTAR

On the high altar is a notable 9th-century ★**altar casing** [**H**] by the German goldsmith Volvinius. The front shows the Redeemer, the symbols of the Evangelists, the Apostles and the Life of Christ;

on the back are scenes from the life of St Ambrose. Above the altar is a notable 9th-century ★ **ciborium**. The impressive Lombard-Byzantine baldachin, also from the 9th century, is decorated with gilt and polychrome stucco and, clockwise from the front, depicts: *Christ Giving the Keys to Peter and the Book to Paul*, *The Virgin and Two Worshippers*, *Sts Ambrose, Gervase and Protasius Receiving the Model of the Ciborium* and *St Benedict with Two Believers*.

THE APSE

Around the raised apse [**I**] are several sections off the double row of choir stalls dating from the 16th century, with carvings depicting scenes from the life of St Ambrose; at the centre is a marble episcopal chair from the 9th century. The mosaics in the apse depict: *Christ with Sts Gervase and Protasius* and, on the left, *St Ambrose at the Burial of St Martin of Tours* and, on the right, *Sts Ambrose and Augustine*.

THE CRYPT

Beneath the choir is the **crypt**. The first chamber is decorated in the baroque style of the 18th century, while the second contains a silver shrine (1898) containing the relics of Sts Ambrose, Gervase and Protasius. At the back of this room is

Star Attraction
● **Sant'Ambrogio**

 Crowning glory
An impressive roll-call of nine emperors were crowned with the 'Iron Crown of the Lombards' in the basilica of Sant'Ambrogio. The first was Otto I, the first Holy Roman emperor, crowned king of Italy in 951. The crown itself, which is in fact made not of iron but of gold – an iron nail believed to have come from the True Cross is fixed in the crown – dates from the 5th century and is now kept in the cathedral in Monza *(see pages 91–2)*.

Sant'Ambrogio

Maps on
pages
48 & 64

Torre Branca

This elegant metal tower, built by Gio Ponti, Cesare Chiodi and Ettore Ferrari in 1933 as part of the Triennale exhibition, stands 108m (354ft) high and is located on Viale Camoens, just a short walk from Cadorna. The tower was closed from 1972 but was recently restored courtesy of Milan's Fratelli Branca liquor distillery and is now open to the public again. Magnificent views can be had from the top platform, 97m (318ft) above the ground.

Capella della Santa Sevina, Sant'Ambrogio

a porphyry sarcophagus in which the relics were discovered in 1864 and the Colonna della Pietà, which once stood in Piazza Castello to mark the site of the martyrdom of Gervase and Protasius.

Highlights in the crypt include the 5th-century *Sacello di San Vittore in Ciel d'Oro* [J] *(see plan on page 64)*, the ceiling of which features St Victor, with (to the right of him) Sts Felix, Maternus and Nabor and (to the left) saints Ambrose, Gervase and Protasius. Also of note is the Capella della Santa Sevina [K] with an Early Christian sarcophagus (5th century), which depicts scenes from the Passion and acts as an altarpiece.

On the architrave above the doors is *Putti Picking Grapes* [L], a rare work dating from the 5th or 6th century. A little further on, the baptistry has a *Resurrection* fresco by Bergognone (1491).

At the altar [M] in the chapel is a round painting of the Madonna by Luini. Further towards the altar is the tomb-slab [N] of Pippin, second son of Charlemagne. At [O] is the Portico della Canonica, a section of the cloister that was begun by Bramante in 1492 and never completed. The brick building in front of it is the 10th-century Oratorio di San Sigismondo. In the middle of the arcade there are relief busts of Lodovico il Moro and his wife Beatrice; these date from the late 15th century.

MUSEO DELLA BASILICA

The basilica's museum, the ★ **Museo della Basilica di Sant'Ambrogio** (open Wed–Mon 10am–noon and 3–5pm; Sat and Sun 3–5pm), containing treasures amassed over the centuries and relics that date back to the basilica's earliest times, has recently been rehoused in the Museo Diocesano and the San Vittore in Ciel d'Oro, with some works in the Antico Oratorio della Passione (Piazza Sant'Ambrogio 23a).

In the middle of the Piazza Sant'Ambrogio is the Tempio della Vittoria (1928, by Muzio), commemorating the Milanese who fell during World War I. At the southern end of the square is the Colonna del Diavolo, an antique column, which derives its name from a local legend. You will notice two holes in the column, and it is said that they were left by the devil's horns when he was angered at his discovery that St Ambrose was not to be tempted.

Below: Campanile dei Canonici, Sant'Ambrogio
Bottom: Sant'Ambrogio

TOWARDS THE CIRCO ROMANO

Beyond the basilica is the **Università Cattólica del Sacro Cuore** ❸❺ (open Mon–Fri 8am–9.30pm and Sat 8am–4.30pm during university term only), Milan's Catholic university. Founded in 1921, it is housed in a former monastery dating from 789; it was originally occupied by Benedictines, then was subsequently handed to monks of the Cistercian Order in 1497 and then dissolved in 1797. The two cloisters and the assembly hall (formerly the refectory) are by Bramante; the latter contains *The Wedding at Cana*, a 16th-century fresco by Callisto Piazza.

If time allows, a quick visit to **San Bernardino** ❸❻ in Via Lanzone is very rewarding; the little church of received its present-day appearance in 1428 and the interior contains 15th-century Lombard frescoes.

Not far away, in the courtyard of the house at Via Torchio 16, the remains of a section of the ancient **Circo Romano** ❸❼ can still be seen. The Roman circus is thought to have originally accommodated around 30,000 spectators.

Map opposite

Biblioteca Ambrosiana
Within the Palazzo dell' Ambrosiana is the Biblioteca Ambrosiana (Mon–Fri 9.30am–5pm). Opened in 1609, the library comprises around 900,000 volumes and 35,000 manuscripts. Its most valuable possessions are fragments of the *Iliad*, a book by Virgil with annotations by Petrarch, a Gothic Bible and the Codice Atlantico, a collection of drawings by Leonardo da Vinci. A stone tablet in the library warns that the penalty for stealing a volume is instant excommunication.

San Sepolcro

6: Around the Pinacoteca Ambrosiana

Slightly to the west of Piazza del Duomo is Milan's financial area, Milano finanziario, with the city's stock exchange on Piazza Affari. Near here is one of Milan's most distinguished art collections, housed in the Palazzo dell'Ambrosiana and the focal point of this tour. Allow at least a couple of hours to visit the museum.

PIAZZA BORROMEO

The tour starts at Piazza Borromeo, where the Milanese family of the same name used to hold tournaments. In the centre of the piazza, note the 17th-century copper statue of San Carlo Borromeo by Bussola. In 1943 the area around the square was badly damaged during an air raid, especially the **Casa dei Borromei** ❸❽, the family's palace, which was home to Milanese cardinals Carlo Borromeo (1538–84) and Federico Borromeo (1564–1631). Today's building is a reconstruction of the former one, and use was made of as many of the original 15th-century fragments as possible. Interesting features here include the pointed-arch portal, the Lombard Gothic court of honour and the gaming hall adjoining the courtyard, which contains some very fine 15th-century frescoes.

SAN SEPOLCRO

Proceed along Via Bollo now as far as the Piazza di San Sepolcro, the site of the old Roman forum. The baths lay on the southern side of the piazza; the Palazzo Castani (18th century) was built above their foundations. Opposite the palazzo is the church of **San Sepolcro** ❸❾ (open daily noon–2pm). Consecrated to the Holy Sepulchre in 1040, this church received its present-day appearance in the 12th and 14th century; the interior has been re-modelled in baroque style. A 14th-century sarcophagus in the crypt contains various relics captured by the Milanese during the Second Crusade (1147–49).

PALAZZO DELL'AMBROSIANA

Beyond the church is the Piazza Pio XI, which is dominated by the **Palazzo dell'Ambrosiana**. The palace was constructed between 1603 and 1609 by Lelio Buzzi to house the library and painting collection that Cardinal Federico Borromeo began in 1595. The ground floor houses the **Biblioteca Ambrosiana** *(see box, opposite)*, while on the upper storey is the impressive art collection.

PINACOTECA AMBROSIANA

The ★★**Pinacoteca Ambrosiana** (open Tues–Sun 10am–5.30pm, last entry one hour prior to closing time) picture gallery, which was extensively restored and elegantly reorganised for the new millennium, showcases one of the most important collections in Milan, including many paintings of the Lombard and Venetian schools. The following gives details of the various rooms in the gallery, noting their main artworks.

FIRST FLOOR

The visit starts on the first floor, with paintings from the collection of Cardinal Federico Borromeo. Over 170 paintings were donated by Borromeo in total, many of which form the pick of the gallery. Highlights in Room 1 include works by Luini and Titian's *Adoration of the Magi*.

Star Attraction
● Pinacoteca Ambrosiana

Statue of Carlo Borromeo, Piazza Borromeo

Map on page 69

Five days in 1848
After the fall of Napoleon, the Congress of Vienna of 1814–15 reaffirmed Austria's claims to Lombardy. However, in 1848, with the support of the Sardinian Royal House, the House of Savoy, the leaders of the Italian Unity Movement (the Risorgimento) ousted the Austrians from Milan for five days, between the 18 and 22 March. After a short period of liberty, the Austrians won the region back, remaining in power there for a further 11 years (until 1859).

Room 2 focuses on Italian paintings of the 15th and 16th centuries, including Ghirlandaio's tondo of the Nativity, Leonardo Da Vinci's *Portrait of a Musician*, Boticelli's *Madonna of the Pavilion*, Pinturicchio's *Madonna with Child* and Bellini's *Adoration of the Infant Jesus with St John*. Room 3 covers Lombard painters of the 15th and 16th centuries, such as Marco d'Oggiono, Bramantino, Luini and Salaino. These paintings are not from the collection of Federico Borromeo.

Rooms 4, 5, 6 and 7, however, feature further works from the Borromeo collection. Highlights are: in Room 4, paintings by Titian and Bassano's *Rest on the Flight into Egypt;* in Room 5, the cartoon *School of Athens* by Raphael; and, in Room 6, *Basket of Fruit* by Caravaggio.

There is a shift in mood in Rooms 7 and 8, where the work of painters from outside Italy is on show. Room 7 is dedicated to Flemish masters, with an impressive range of works by Jan Brueghel the Elder set alongside paintings by Paul Brill. Room 8 contains works from the 14th to 16th centuries.

By Room 9, however, the stress is back on Italy, notably paintings and objects from the 15th and 16th centuries. Venetian masters of the 16th century including Moretto and Tintoretto are on show in Rooms 10 and 12, while Room 11 contains Italian masters of the 15th and 16th centuries, notably a portrait of a man by Bronzino.

SECOND FLOOR

Now head upstairs towards Room 13, which continues the visit with Italian and Flemish masters of the 16th and 17th centuries. Artists showcased include Salvator Rosa, Luca Giordano and Victorian favourite Guido Reni, whose wonderfully delicate *Madonna* deserves careful consideration. In Rooms 14 are Italian masters of the 17th century, while Rooms 15 and 16 concentrate on Lombardy. Examples of 17th-century Lombard masters such as Vermiglio, Procaccini and Crespi are shown in both rooms; works from the 18th century, including paintings by Tiepolo, Magnasco and Fra'Galgario, are displayed in Room 17.

The De Pacis Collection of neoclassical bronzes is on show in Room 18. Also in this room is a proud self-portrait by Canova.

The final room on this floor (19) is home to works by Italian masters of the 19th and early 20th centuries including Appiani, Hayez, Migliara, Induno, Mosè Bianchi, Previati and Gola.

At this point, you can return downstairs, to the gallery shop, via Room 20, the tiny fountained atrium-like peristyle. Sala Luini (Room 24) is on the ground floor.

SAN SATIRO

The route now continues along Via Asole to Via Torino; by taking a southerly direction down this street you will come to the early baroque church of **San Sebastiano**, constructed in 1577 according to designs by Pellegrino Tibaldi. Continue north from here and you will reach the ★★**Basilica di San Satiro** ⓐ (Via Torino 5, tel: 02-7202 1804; open Mon–Sat 8.30–11.30am, 3.30–5.30pm, Sun 9.30–10.30am and 4.30–5.30pm; note that San Satiro is often closed for restoration, so it's advisable to telephone ahead to check it's open before you visit). The church, which is one of the most important architectural monuments in Milan, is named after St Satirus, the brother of the city's patron saint, Ambrose.

Star Attraction
● San Satiro

Below: Ambrosiana portrait
Bottom: Basket of Fruit
by Caravaggio

Maps
on page
69 and
opposite

HISTORY

Founded in the 9th century and consecrated by
Archbishop Heribert of Intimiano in 1036, San
Satiro was rebuilt in Renaissance style in 1478
by Bramante. The 9th-century baptistry on Via
Mazzini, which had been completely separate
from the rest of the church until then, was given
a Renaissance exterior by Bramante and incorporated into the transept as the Cappella della
Pietà. The main façade was begun by the architect Amadeo in 1486 according to designs by Bramante; however, construction was exceptionally
slow, and the façade was not fully completed until
1871. The Romanesque brick campanile next to
the church is also a 9th-century structure and is
the oldest Romanesque belltower in Lombardy.

San Satiro

THE INTERIOR

The interior of the church is actually T-shaped,
but Bramante's clever use of perspective and
stucco, most notably the introduction of a false
apse, create the allusion that the it is in the shape
of a Greek cross. The neoclassical high altar gains
greatly from this arrangement.

The much-revered votive fresco of the
Madonna and Child at the altar was originally
located outside the church; blood is said to have
issued from the painting when a certain Maz-
zanzio da Vigolzone flung a knife at it in 1242,
and since then it has been credited with miracu-
lous powers. Above the arches in the nave and
extending into the transepts is a remarkable frieze;
the coffered dome dates from 1483. The spandrels
contain the 16th-century *Evangelists* by the
school of Vincenzo Foppa, a Milanese painter
who was strongly influenced by Bellini.

The entrance leading to the magnificent sacristy is located to the right of the main portal. The
coloured terracotta frieze here is by Agostino de
Fondutis, based on designs by Bramante. To the
left of the high altar is the Cappella della Pietà
(mentioned above), which is home to a polychrome terracotta *Pietà* dating from *circa* 1482
and by de Fondutis.

7: East of the Duomo

This tour explores the part of the city centre directly east of the Duomo and Palazzo Reale – an area that you may wish to explore if you're spending more than a few days in the city.

TOWARD SAN BERNADINO

Start the tour at Piazza Fontana, just behind the Palazzo Reale *(see page 23)*. On the eastern side of the square is the former **Palazzo dei Tribunali** or **Palazzo del Capitano di Giustizia** ❷, the Palace of Justice *(see box right)*.

To the south, on Piazza Santo Stefano, is the basilica after which this square is named; on the left is the **Santuario di San Bernardino dei Monti** ❸ (open daily 7.30am–1pm). This octagonal church was built in the 12th century and given its present-day baroque appearance in 1750. The covered walk in front of the building first leads to an ossuary, filled with human skulls and bones. Legend has it that these are the bones of Milanese Catholics who lost their lives in the battles with the Aryans during St Ambrose's time. In fact, they are probably the bones brought here from the former cemetery of Santo Stefano. The skulls in the boxes above the door are said to have been those of condemned men. The fresco in the vault is by Sebastiano Ricci (1695).

City jurisdiction
Constructed between 1605 and 1750, Milan's Palazzo dei Tribunali (Palace of Justice) was used to house the city's chief magistrates. Sentences and proclamations were made from the balcony above the main entrance, and Milan's chief executioner resided close to all matters of life and death in a room below the roof. In later years the building was also used as a court; nowadays it is used by the Polizia Municipale (Vigili Urbane).

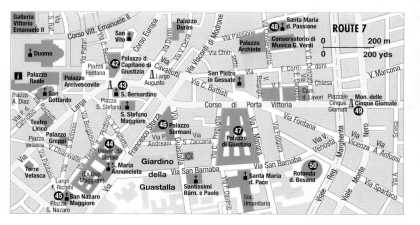

UNIVERSITÀ STATALE

Along the nearby Via del Perdono is the former Ospedale Maggiore Sforzesco, now the ★ **Università Statale ⑭**. The right wing of this brick building, the city's first ever hospital, was begun in 1457 under Francesco Sforza according to plans by Filarete; work continued after 1465 under Guiniforte Solari and Giovanni Antonio Amadeo. The architectural style is a mixture of Gothic and Renaissance. Filarete provided the ground floor with a series of arcades on a raised plinth; the upper storey, by Solari, with its pointed-arch double windows, rests on a richly decorated cornice. The brick decor is late 15th-century Lombard; the marble busts in the spandrels of the arcades are 17th-century additions. The raised central section of the building and the inner courtyard were both built by Richini in 1624 and harmonise well with the right wing of the church (the first part to be built). The rather uninspiring left wing was added between 1798 and 1804.

The hospital was shifted from here in 1939, and then restored after the bomb damage of 1943; today it houses Milan University's faculties of Philosophy, Letters and Law.

Below: sculpture on the façade of the Università Statale
Bottom: stained glass, Capella Trivulzio, San Nazaro Maggiore

SAN NAZARO MAGGIORE

To the southeast of the Università Statale is ★ **San Nazaro Maggiore ⑮** (open daily 7.30am–noon and 3–6.30pm). This 4th-century church was built on the site of an Early Christian basilica, and destroyed by a fire in 1075. It is entered via the Cappella Trivulzio (1512, by Bramantino), the funeral chapel of the Trivulzio family. On the left-hand wall, on either side of the altar, are valuable frescoes: on the left, an early 15th-century *Madonna and Child with St Matronianus* and, on the right, the 13th-century fresco, *Christ Appears to Mary Magdalene*. The left transept provides access to the large *Cappella di Santa Caterina* (1540), with its fine painted glass depicting scenes from the life of the saint; also here is a German *Adoration* (16th century) and the fresco *Martyrdom of St Catherine* by Lanino (1546).

The right transept contains two Pre-Romanesque niches dating back to the original structure; the right-hand one houses a 16th-century copy of Gaudenzio Ferrari's *Last Supper*, while the one on the left contains a 15th-century bas-relief of the *Crucifixion* by Bonino da Campione. The right transept also provides access to the sacristy, home to a 5th-century, early Christian silver shrine.

PALAZZO SORMANI

Passing the modern clinic buildings along Via Francesco Sforza, the route now leads to the magnificent **Palazzo Sormani** ㊻. The baroque façade of this palazzo was created by Francesco Croce in 1736; the side facing the garden is neoclassical (1756, by Benedetto Alfieri). Today the palazzo houses the Biblioteca Sormani, which, with over a million volumes, is Milan's largest library. Behind the palace, in Via Francesco Sforza, are the delightful **Giardini della Guastalla** (Guastalla Gardens), which were laid out in 1555.

The Big House
Owing to its huge dimensions (the length of the façade alone is 265m/875ft) the complex of the Università Statale is known familiarly as Ca'Granda (The Big House).

PALAZZO DI GIUSTIZIA

Continue eastwards up the broad Corso di Porta Vittoria, and on the right is the enormous **Palazzo di Giustizia** ㊼ (Palace of Justice). Designed by Piacentini, this grand building, with its 120-m

Art deco design, Palazzo di Giustizia

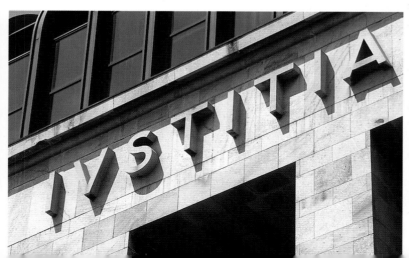

Map on page 73

(395-ft) long façade, is typical of the Facist architecture of the decade prior to World War II. The trapezoid ground-plan has a large courtyard of honour, 12 smaller courtyards and over 100 rooms. The courtrooms are partly decorated with sculptures, frescoes and modern mosaics.

Torre Velasca
Located almost directly south of the Duomo is this reinforced concrete, brutalist-style skyscraper, designed by Studio BBPR, the Milanese architectural group of Banfi, Belgiojoso, Peressutti & Rogers, in the late 1950s. The firm's work combines strong influence of both the Bauhaus (clean, pure lines) and traditional Italian architectural styles – the cantilevered upper section, for example, is strongly reminiscent of the design of a traditional Italian fortress.

SAN PIETRO IN GESSATE

Opposite the Palazzo di Giustizia is the 15th-century **San Pietro in Gessate** (open daily 8am–6pm). Probably built by Guiniforte Solari, the church was later partly renovated in baroque style. Beyond is Via Filippo Corridoni; follow this street to the right as far as the Via Conservatorio, then turn down the latter. House No 1 here is the former monastery of the Lateran Order, which is now home to the Giuseppe Verdi Conservatoire and Concert Hall, founded in 1808. The magnificent early Renaissance pillared courtyard, built in the first decades of the 16th century, is attributed to Cristoforo Solari.

SANTA MARIA DELLA PASSIONE

Next door is the church of ★ **Santa Maria della Passione** ⓮ (open daily 7am–noon and 3–6pm). Construction work began on this church in 1485, and between 1511 and 1530 it was given its mighty

Detail, Santa Maria della Passione

dome by Cristoforo Solari. The nave and the baroque façade, with its reliefs depicting scenes from the Passion, date from 1692. The pillars lining the interior are decorated with paintings depicting saints and monks of the Lateran Order; these date from 1622 and are by Daniele Crespi. The scenes from the Passion at the foot of the pilasters beneath the cupola are also by Crespi. Look out, in the Chapel of the Crucifixion, for the magnificent *Entombment* (1516) by Bernardino Luini.

MONUMENTO DELLE CINQUE GIORNATE

After visiting this church go back to the Corso di Porta Vittoria and follow it along the left-hand side as far as the Piazzale Cinque Giornati and the **Monumento delle Cinque Giornate 49**. This monument, created by Giuseppe Grandi in 1895, commemorates the 'Five Days' Uprising' *(see box, page 70)*. It consists of a 22-m (73-ft) high bronze obelisk bearing the names of the patriots who fell. The obelisk is surrounded by five female figures, symbolising the five days, and a lion and eagle. The bell, a copy of the tower bell on the Piazza Mercanti, bears the inscription, 'Though Immobile, I Still Sound.' A crypt beneath the monument contains the bones of those who fell.

ROTONDA DELLA BESANA

Now turn right, up Viale Regina Margherita. On the corner of Via San Barnaba is the most original 18th-century building in Milan, the **Rotonda della Besana 50**. This was actually the former ceme-tery of the Ospedale Maggiore *(see page 74)* and was built by Francesco Raffagno between 1698 and 1725. The church, with its four wings and its octagonal central section crowned by a dome, is encircled by a harmoniously laid out cloister. In 1809 Napoleon's stepson, the Viceroy of Italy, Eugène de Beauharnais, wanted to turn the build-ing into a Pantheon of the Italian Empire, but the plan was not carried out for financial reasons. There is an open-air cinema here in summer.

Rotonda della Besana

Map
below

8: The Fashion District

There are few things with which Milan is more synonymous than fashion, and this route takes you through the pedestrian shopping area around the Duomo right into the heart of the upmarket fashion quarter to the northeast. Here, the great houses of Armani, Prada and Versace sit side by side with up-and-coming catwalk designers. Should your budget allow, you can kit yourself out at Etro, try on some Ferragamo shoes and complete the outfit with this season's Louis Vuitton clutch bag. The tour ends at Milan's most attractive green space, the Giardini Pubblici, also home to the Villa Reale art gallery.

CORSO VITTORIO EMANUELE II

Polish your shoes, pull on your glad-rags and start at the rear of the Duomo, from where Corso Vittorio Emanuele II leads to Piazza San Babila. The Corso, originally laid down by the Romans, was Milan's top fashion promenade in the 19th century and is still one of the city's most popular commercial thoroughfares today. Rebuilt after suffering serious bomb damage in 1943, the buildings along the Corso have high arcades and house elegant shops. Most of the stores along here, however, are high-street names – the designers are located slightly further northeast.

SAN CARLO AL CORSO

At the end of the Corso, on the left and set slightly back from the street, is the church of **San Carlo al Corso** ⑤. This round, neoclassical structure was built in 1838 by Carlo Amati and is consecrated to San Carlo Borromeo, cardinal of Milan. Beyond a pillared portico is the mighty dome (interior diameter 32m/106ft) plated with copper. Inside the church on the left of the entrance is a 15th-century Lombard relief, *Bishop with Crib*.

SAN BABILA

The Corso now broadens out into Piazza San Babila, which is also joined by the elegant Corso Matteotti. Opposite is the ancient **Basilica di San Babila** ⓬ (open Mon–Sat 7.30am–noon and 3.30–7pm; Sun 7.30–1.15pm and 4.30–7pm). This restored Romanesque church was built in the 5th century on the site of a pagan temple; it was renewed in the 11th century, and then altered several times. The side façades, with their characteristic flying buttresses, and the domed crossing, with its openings for *logge,* best convey the building's original appearance. The fresco and mosaic decoration in the interior is almost completely modern. An inscription inside the church states that the poet Alessandro Manzoni was baptised here on 8 August 1785. In front of the church is the Colonna del Leone (Lion's Column), which was placed here to commemorate a Milanese victory over the Venetians.

Versace

For the flash and famous, one label reigns supreme — that of the late Gianni Versace. Originally from the south, he moved to Milan at the age of 25 and began to design; his only training being from his mother. His first collection was presented in 1978, and he soon established his signature skimpy and sexually-charged style. Synonymous with the cult of the supermodel, he was surrounded by a nexus of wealth and fame, and his murder in Miami in 1997 caused shock and horror in the fashion world, until his sister, Donatella, the embodiment of the Versace style, stepped in to save the label.

QUADRILATERO DELLA MODA

From the Piazza San Babila you now head to what is known as Milan's *Quadrilatero della moda*, or fashion quadrilateral, incorporating vias Montenapoleone, Mazoni, Sant'Andrea and della Spiga. For the budget-conscious majority, shopping here is likely to be of the window variety

Sign of a major fashion street

MONTENAPOLEONE

Map on page 78

only. However, those with sufficient funds can do serious damage to their bank accounts in elegant designer stores from Cartier, Chanel, Dolce e Gabbana and Etro to Fendi, Ferragamo, Hermès, Jil Sander, Moschino, Prada, Valentino and Versace, to name but a few. The *palazzo* with the magnificent inner courtyard in Via Gesù belonged to the late Gianni Versace, whose boutique is at Via Montenapoleone 2.

Below and bottom:
shopping alla Milanese

MUSEO DI MILANO

For those looking for something other than fashion, the **Museo di Milano** ㊼ (open Tues–Sun 9am–1pm, 2–6pm) is also on Via Sant'Andrea, at No 6. The recently restored municipal museum, housed in the delightful 18th-century Palazzo Morando, documents the development of Milan and features a chronological exhibition of furniture, paintings, engravings, coins, medals and other items. The building also houses the **Museo di Storia Contemporanea** (Museum of Contemporary History).

PALAZZO BAGATTI-VALSECCHI

The route now follows Via Montenapoleone as far as Via Santo Spirito (note Valentino at No 3). At No 10 is the huge **Palazzo Bagatti-Valsecchi**

(open Tues–Sun 1–5.45pm). Built in neo-Renaissance style in the 19th century, the palace contains a small art collection. In the courtyard is the *Madonna del Ratt*, so named in Milanese dialect because the infant Jesus is carrying a mouse on his shoulder.

CASA FONTANA

Via Santo Spirito leads on to Via della Spiga, where Versace is at No 4 and Krizia is at No 23; Via della Spiga takes you to Corso Venezia. The building at No 11 that housed the former priests' seminary is worth a closer look: it was built in 1564 and has a magnificent baroque portal by Richini (17th century).

Opposite is the dignified ★ **Casa Fontana** (54), the oldest building on Corso Venezia and generally considered to be one of the best-preserved and most typical 15th-century patrician residences in all Milan. The Casa's façade (*circa* 1475) still retains the characteristic grace of the Lombard Renaissance and reveals the influence of Bramante. Finely worked columns shaped like candelabra adorn the main portal, and the windows have fine brick decoration.

Innate style

In addition to its fashion success, Milan is also widely acknowledged to be the design capital of Italy. Fashion guru Anna Piaggi once remarked, 'It helps to have been born in Milan: it's a graphic city, dedicated to good design, but also deeply surrealistic.'

Arrmani, Via Montenapoleone

PALAZZO SERBELLONI

A few steps further on the right is the enormous **Palazzo Serbelloni** (55). Construction on this magnificent palazzo in the city's eastern suburbs commenced in 1760, but after a pause in the building work it was finished in the neoclassical style by Ticino architect Simone Cantoni for the counts of Serbelloni. Napoleon Bonaparte lived here in 1796, as did Vittorio Emanuele II in 1859. The long bas-relief frieze (by F. and D. Carabelli) stretching along the façade depicts the history of the Lombard League. Today the palazzo is used by the Milan press club.

Situated further along Corso Venezia, at No 40 and on the right, is the impressive **Palazzo Rocca-Saporiti**, constructed by Giuseppe Perego in 1812 and generally considered to be one of

Map on page 78

the city's finest neoclassical buildings. The elegant sculptural decoration, by Pompeo Marchesi and Giorgio Rusca, is especially fine.

PALAZZO DEL SENATO

Taking a different street at the Palazzo Serbelloni, Via Senato leads past the church of San Pietro Celestino, mostly built in 1735 but with a 14th-century campanile, and to **Palazzo del Senato ⑤⑥**. This palace was commissioned from Fabio Mangone in 1620 by Cardinal Federico Borromeo; it was completed by Richini and initially served as a *Collegio Svizzero*, a seminary for Swiss priests. During the Napoleonic Kingdom of Italy (1809–14) it housed the Senate. Today it contains the state archives.

Façade, Villa Reale

VILLA REALE

Opposite the Palazzo del Senato is a park laid out with English-style gardens, a small lake and a fountain (by A. Wildt); these are the grounds of the **Villa Reale ⑤⑦** (Via Palestro 16). This royal villa was built by Viennese architect Leopold Pollak in 1790 for the counts of Barbiano di Belgioioso. The main façade, which is typically neoclassical, faces the park, while the entrance faces the Via Palestro and the Giardini Pubblici (*see opposite*). In 1803 the villa was purchased by the Cisalpine Republic and presented to Napoleon I, who lived here with Josephine; a stepson of Napoleon's, Eugène de Beauharnais, Viceroy of Italy, resided here too. In 1858 the Austrian field-marshal Count Joseph Radetzky died here; he had been commander-in-chief of the imperial troops in Italy from 1831 to 1857.

In 1859 the building passed into the hands of the House of Savoy, and since 1919 has been the property of the City of Milan, which installed a **Civica Galleria d'Arte Moderna** here in 1921 (open Tues–Sun 9am–5.30pm). The grand salon of the villa is of particular interest; its ceiling has a fresco of *Apollo and the Muses* by Andrea Appiani (1811).

GIARDINI PUBBLICI

On the other side of Via Palestro, between Piazza Cavour and the Porta Venezia, is Milan's most attractive green space, the ★ **Giardini Pubblici**. The park covers an area of almost 18 hectares (44 acres) and was originally laid out in 1782 by Piermarini, who made use of the grounds of former monasteries. The gardens were given their present-day appearance in 1858 by Giuseppe Balzaretti, who designed them in the English romantic style, with bushes, small hills, ponds and an abundance of exotic plants. West of the park is the **Palazzo Dugnani** 🟡**58**, the main hall of which is decorated with frescoes by Giovanni Battista (Giambattista) Tiepolo; the palace contains Milan's **Museo del Cinema**.

Also in the park is the **Museo Civico di Storia Naturale** 🟡**59** (open Mon–Fri 9am–6pm, Sat and Sun 9.30am–6.30pm), Milan's Natural History Museum. Founded in 1838, the museum is housed inside a neo-Romanesque/Gothic building dating from 1893. The ground floor contains mineral collections and palaeontological exhibits, including a huge 40-kilo (88-lb) topaz, a collection of meteorites and a dinosaur skeleton. The zoological collection and the library are on the first floor. East of the park, past the children's playground and the **Planetario di Milano** 🟡**60** (Planetarium) is Porta Venezia metro station.

Modern art
Although the main bulk of the collection of the Giardini Pubblici's Galleria d'Arte Moderna *(see opposite)* has now been incorporated into the Museo d'Arte Contemporanea in the Palazzo Reale *(see page 23)*, among the art still on show at the Civica Galleria are several works by Marino Marini and the Vismara and Grassi collections, which include paintings by Van Gogh, Cézanne, Corot and other important 19th-century artists.

Statues in the Giardini Pubblici

Map opposite

Below: Basilica di San Lorenzo Maggiore
Middle: Basilica di Sant'Eustorgio
Bottom: Colonne di San Lorenzo

9: The Navigli

This route goes south of the city centre to the trendy canal quarter, the *Navigli* (canals); the district comes alive in the evenings (after around 10pm), when the proliferation of bars and restaurants overlooking the canal opens its doors to the Milanese and to tourists alike. During the daytime, the area can seem oddly deserted (except on market day, *see below*), so if you want to catch the canals at their most atmospheric and are not concerned about seeing the interior of the churches listed, try this route at night.

If you want to visit the interiors of the churches listed below, make a morning or afternoon visit to the *Navigli*. It's best to do this on market days, when bric-a-brac, antiques and food are touted here with stereotypical Italian flair. On Saturdays, the Darsena canal, near to Porta Genova, and the Naviglio Grande bustle with the Fiera di Senigallia, where stallholders display bric-a-brac along the canalside. The Mercatone del Naviglio Grande, held on the last Sunday of every month, is a rather more lavish affair, with more upmarket wares on offer to discerning Milanese shoppers.

COLONNE DI SAN LORENZO

To reach the starting point of the tour from Piazza del Duomo, walk down Via Torino southwestwards as far as the long square known as Carrobbio; from there to take the broad Corso di Porta Ticinese southwards. On the left are the antique **Colonne di San Lorenzo** ❻. These 16 columns once formed part of either a Roman temple or a complex of thermal baths dating from the 2nd or 3rd century AD. They were placed here in the 4th century as an entrance portico for the church beyond.

SAN LORENZO MAGGIORE

The ★★**Basilica di San Lorenzo Maggiore** ❻, built on Roman foundations, probably originated as an Aryan basilica *circa* AD350, becoming a

Catholic church at the time of St Ambrose. The ceiling collapsed twice after conflagrations in the 11th and 12th centuries and was renewed in the Lombard Romanesque style. In 1573 the dome collapsed yet again and was reconstructed in the Late Renaissance style by Martino Bassi.

Star Attractions
● **the Navigli**
● **Basilica di San Lorenzo Maggiore**

PORTA TICINESE AND THE DARSENA

The route now continues along the Corso di Porta Ticinese, passing **Porta Ticinese** ㊿, an ancient city gate that formed part of the city wall erected in 1171 after the destruction of Milan by Barbarossa. Traditionally, all the important people in the city would enter by Porta Ticanese, and even today, newly elected archbishops still take this route into Milan. On the outside of the gate is a relief (*circa* 1330) by the Pisan artist Giovanni di Balduccio. It portrays the *Madonna and Saints, with St Ambrose Handing Over the Model of the City.*

Canal history
Until the 1970s, Milan was Italy's third-largest port in terms of tonnage, and barges carrying sand and gravel travelled into the city along the canals. The Naviglio Grande, which leads more than 50km (30 miles) to the River Ticino, was built in the 14th century. The Naviglio Pavese, built by the Visconti family and measuring 33km (20 miles), saw more then 1,400 barges travel along its narrow strip each year.

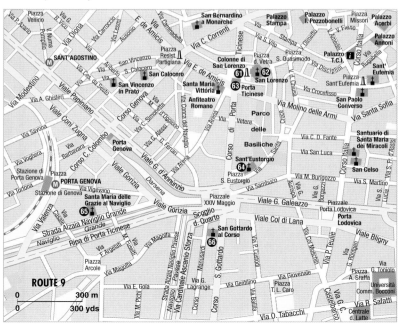

Maps on
page 85
and
below

Cappella Portinari

This chapel, commissioned by the banker Pigello Portinari and created by the Florentine artist Michelozzo Michelozzi between 1462 and 1466, is one of the finest examples of Renaissance art in Milan. The chapel was built to house the relics of St Peter Martyr, which were contained in a lavish Carrara marble sarcophagus, and as Portinari's own resting place. The silver reliquary in a small chapel to the left of the altar contains the skull of the saint.

To the west of Porta Ticinese is the **Darsena**, formerly Milan's old harbour basin but now the gateway to the heart of Milanese nightlife in this area. One of the best views of the canals can be had from the green kiosk on the Darsena. Bargain hunters should note that the Fiera di Sinigallia *(see page 84)* is held here on Saturdays.

SANT'EUSTORGIO

Follow Corso di Porta Ticinese further south; at the end on the left is the little Piazza Sant'Eustorgio. Beyond it is the restored ★★ **Basilica di Sant' Eustorgio** ❻ (open daily 7.30am–noon, 3.30–6.30pm). The basilica was built in the 11th century on the site of an oratory founded by Bishop Eustorgius; according to legend the oratory contained the relics of the Three Magi, presented to the bishop by the Emperor Constantine. The exterior of the church has changed much over the centuries, reflecting styles from Gothic to Baroque.

Highlights inside the church include private chapels of the Brivio [1] *(see plan, left)*, Tommaso [2], Visconti [3 and 5] and Portinari [10] families. Also of note are a late 16th-century *Madonna, Child and Saints* [4], attributed to Cerano, two 14th-century sarcophagi [6] and the Cappella dei Magi (Chapel of the Wise Men) [7]. On the 14th-century high altar are large marble panels [8] showing scenes from the passion that are generally considered to be the finest marble work of this period in Milan. Inside the 16th-century Sacristy [9] are magnificent baroque cabinets.

**SANT'
EUSTORGIO**

10 Cappella Portinari

9 Sacristy

7 Cappella dei Magi
8 Marble panel
6 Sarcophagi

5 Cappella Visconti

4 *Madonna, Child and Saints*

3 Cappella dei Visconti

2 Cappella dei Tommaso

1 Cappella dei Brivio

THE NAVIGLIO GRANDE

Now walk along the right bank of the Naviglio Grande and you'll soon reach the remains of the **Vicolo dei Lavanda**, the old wash-houses that used to line the bank of the canal. The steps and stone slabs on which the women of the quarter scrubbed their laundry can still be seen on the bank.

Beyond the late 19th-century church of **Santa Maria delle Grazie al Naviglio** 🔵 is a small bridge above the canal, where you can stand and look over the quirky shops, galleries and restaurants that line the bank. If you turn right here, you'll reach the Stazione di Porta Genova, home to the hip La Scaletta restaurant *(see page 114)*.

If you leave the bridge on the left bank of the canal, the Ripa di Porta Ticinese, however, and turn straight into Via Paoli, you'll arrive at Piazza Arcole. In the summer, you can swim here at the square's **Piscina Argelati** (open daily 10am–7pm), one of the most pleasant open-air pools in the city.

THE NAVIGLIO PAVESE

From Piazza Arcole, follow Via Magolfa towards the slim Naviglio Pavese, built by the Visconti family. If you follow the canal as far as No 15, you can go through a connecting courtyard and emerge at the other side on to Corso San Gottardo, home to the little church of **San Gottardo al Corso** 🔵. The church is especially famed for its elaborate windows.

That culminates your tour of the Navigli. If you're here in the evening celebrate with a drink or meal at one of the district's pleasant watering holes or restaurants.

Star Attractions
● **Basilica di Sant'Eustorgio**
● **the canals at night**

Below: Naviglio Grande
Bottom: Santa Maria Presso San Celso

Map below

Excursions

Milan is the ideal starting-point for brief as well as lengthy excursions into the surrounding Lombard area, the richest and most populous region in Italy with landscapes varying from watery rice paddies to the southeast and soaring mountainous regions to the north. There are good train links to cities including Bergamo, Monza and Pavia and to the Northern Italian lakes (Como and Lecco as well as the lakeside towns of Menaggio and Varenna), and these areas are also very accessible by car. The following section is a starting-point for choosing tours just outside Milan.

BERGAMO

The birthplace of composer Gaetano Donizetti, its name inextricably linked with the lemon-scented oily perfume bergamot, Bergamo is

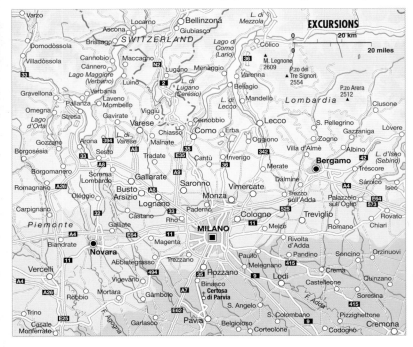

located 50km (30 miles) east of Milan and makes an ideal destination for a day trip. You can take the train from Milan's Stazione Centrale, a coach from Piazza Castello or, if you're driving, take the Autostrada Serenissima (the motorway between Milan and Venice) and come off at the exit for Bergamo; it will take approximately one hour to drive from Milan.

Situated 250m (820ft) above sea level and with a population around 120,000, Bergamo boasts a chequered history. It was a free Imperial City, standing in the fight against Emperor Barbarossa, before falling under Visconti rule; it then spent 400 years as part of the Venetian Republic (hence the proliferation of lions of St Mark across the city), during which time the Venetians turned Bergamo into fortress from which a vast surrounding area could be controlled.

Bergamo consists of two distinct halves: the medieval Bergamo Alta (Upper Town – *alta* means high), lying on a hill and enclosed by a Venetian wall, and the modern Bergamo Bassa (Lower Town – *bassa* means low), with the busy Piazza Vittorio Veneto at its centre.

Below: the view from the Torre Civica
Bottom: Santa Maria Maggiore, Bergamo

BERGAMO ALTA

The picturesque Upper Town can be reached along Viale Vittorio Emanuele via a funicular railway or you can take the virtuous option and walk all the way uphill. Once you reach the Upper Town, the first stop should be the 12th-century **Palazzo della Ragione**, the oldest town hall in Italy. Situated on the Piazza Vecchia, the building has an elegant portico and a Gothic triforium, which features the lion of St Mark.

Close by are the Piazza del Duomo, home to Bergamo's **Duomo** (cathedral). The magnificent edifice was built mostly during the 15th to 17th centuries, although the façade and dome are modern additions. The apse of the cathedral is embellished by a fresco by Tiepolo.

Near to the Duomo is the church of **Santa Maria Maggiore**, built from the 12th to 14th centuries and notable for its baroque interior and, especially, its ★ **Cappella Colleoni**. This magnificent Renaissance chapel was built between 1470 and 1475 as a mausoleum for the Venetian *condottiere* (military leader) Bartolomeo Colleoni and his daughter Meda. Its unusually ornate marble façade is decorated with medallions, while its interior is decorated with 18th-century frescoes by Tiepolo.

Head further up the hill to the town's **Citadella**, the former residence of the Venetian governors, dominated by a massive tower. Once there, pass under a large archway and you'll reach an open square called **Colle Aperto**, the start of the walk up to the **Colli di San Vigilio**, where there is a ruined castle and fabulous views.

Capella Colleoni ceiling, Santa Maria Maggiore, Bergamo

BERGAMO BASSA

Down in Lower Bergamo (you can take a funicular to get back down the hill if you don't fancy repeating the walk), there are several cultural options. Definitely worth a visit is the **Pinacoteca dell'Accademia Carrara**; the gallery contains a superb collection by Bergamo artists including Ghislandi, Bascheni and Lorenzo Lotto, other Italian artists (Botticelli, Raphael, Tintoretto) and international masters (Cranach, Dürer, Rubens, Van Dyck and Vélazquez).

Also in this part of Bergamo is the Teatro Donizetti, named after the great opera composer, who was born and lived in the town. Arguably the most important composer of the 1830s, Donizetti penned such works as *Lucia di Lammermoor* and *L'Elisir d'Amore*. There is a monument to him on the Piazza Cavour, next to the theatre (information from APT, Via Papa Giovanni 106, tel: 035-211020).

If you've been impressed by the work of Lotto (*circa* 1480–1550) – a Venetian artist who settled in Bergamo – make detour to nearby **Trescore** and then drive another a 15km (9 mile) to **Villa Suardi**. Here, in the delightful 14th-century church of **Santa Barbara**, are frescoes by the artist. To return to Milan from here, take the A4 motorway.

MONZA

During medieval times this small town, located approximately 15km (9 miles) to the northwest of Milan (162m/ 530ft above sea level; population around 123,000) was where the Lombard kings were crowned. Nowadays, the town is a fairly industrial affair, with textiles and carpets the major local industries; it's also famed for its motor-racing events.

THE DUOMO

The main architectural highlight in the town is the 14th-century ★ **Duomo di San Giovanni** (open daily 9am–noon, 3–6.30pm), constructed by the architect Matteo da Campione in the Lombard Gothic style on the site of a church founded by the Lombard Queen Theodolinda *(see box on page 92)*. A relief taken from the previous building on this site serves as decoration above the main portal; the frieze depicts the queen, her husband Authari and the Baptism of Christ.

Inside the five-aisled basilica, to the left of the choir, is the ★ **Cappella della Regina Teodolinda** (conducted tours are available; obtain information from the Museo del Duomo, *see page 92)*. Here, on the altar, is the 9th-century 'Iron Crown of the Lombards'. The crown is a headband of beaten gold, studded with precious stones

Below and bottom: views inside Monza's Duomo di San Giovanni

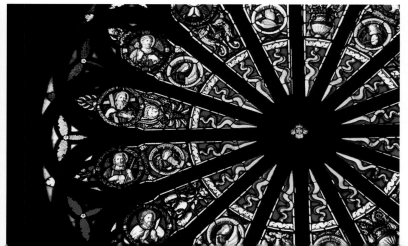

Map on page 88

Queen Theodolinda

In 589 Theodolinda, the daughter of Duke Garibaldo of Bavaria, married the Lombard King Authari. She was well liked among his people, and when Authari died in 590, Theodolinda was made queen in her own right. She remarried and, through her new husband Duke Agilulf of Turin, she established a friendship with Pope Gregory the Great. Her influence on the Arian Lombards was great, converting many to Christianity and building the magnificent Duomo in Monza.

and with an iron rim that is said to have been made from one of the nails of the cross on which Christ died. Thirty-four Lombard monarchs were crowned with it, most recently Charles V (1530), Napoleon (1805) and Ferdinand I of Austria (1836).

The left transept leads on to the Museo del Duomo (open Tues–Sat 9–11.30am and 3–5.30pm), where the rest of the cathedral treasures, including Theodolina's crown, can be admired.

PARCO DI MONZA

The 800-ha (1,977-acre) ★★ **Parco di Monza** extends to the north of the town; its southernmost part is home to the impressive, neoclassical ★ **Villa Reale**, which was built from 1776–80 by Giuseppe Pier Marini and is popularly known as the Versailles of Lombardy. You can visit the interior of the palace, where a collection of 19th-century paintings is housed in the north wing, or, if you prefer to make the most of the gardens, make for the romantic section of park behind the castle, replete with a lake and grottoes. Bicycle hire is available at the entrance on Viale Cavriga, and golf, tennis and swimming are also on offer in the grounds. The park, through which the River Lambro flows, extends a long way north, as far as the *Autodromo*, where national and international motor-racing events are regularly held.

Villa Reale

PAVIA

This small town on the Ticino River, 36km (22 miles) south of Milan and around 10km (6 miles) to the south of the Certosa (77m/250ft above sea-level; population 100,000) has a sort of gloomy magnificence about it. Formerly a Roman settlement, it was later one of the last bastions of the Goths, then a Byzantine fortress, and finally capital of the Lombard Kingdom, remaining so until the 11th century and eclipsing Milan in its importance. Under the Visconti the town became the intellectual and artistic centre of Lombardy, and rivals Bologna as home of the oldest university in Italy (information from APT, Via Fabio Filzi 2, tel: 0382-27238).

Star Attractions
● **Parco di Monza**
● **Duomo, Pavia**

Ponte Vecchio, Pavia

THE DUOMO AND AROUND

The many patricians' houses and palaces situated around the Piazza Municipio at the eastern part of the town testify to Pavia's cultural heritage. The ★★ **Duomo** (1488–1609) is considered the finest example of Lombard Renaissance architecture in Italy, and Bramante, Leonardo da Vinci and Giovanni Amadeo are just a few of the artists who worked on the building. The site was originally occupied by two churches, Santo Stefano and Santa Maria del Popolo; fragments of the former can still be seen next to the ruins of the old Torre Civica that was once attached to the Duomo. This tower, the base of which dates back to the 11th century, collapsed on 17 March 1989, for reasons that are still unclear. The cathedral is the burial place of San Siro, Pavia's first bishop. Its magnificent dome, only completed in 1885, is the third largest in Italy and is the symbol of the town.

The nearby **Basilica di San Michele**, where emperors and kings were crowned during the Middle Ages (including Barbarossa in 1155) is Pavia's oldest Romanesque church. It was founded in 661 and given its present-day appearance in the 12th century. Real highlights here are the façade with its magnificent sculpture decoration, and the huge Romanesque mosaic above the presbytery.

Map on page 88

Local primers

Pavia is famed for its hearty peasant soups *(minestra)*, of which the most celebrated is *zuppa pavese*, a broth with an egg on toast floating on the top – the egg cooks slowly in the broth. This dish was reportedly served to François I, King of France (and of Pavia at that time), to fortify him on the eve of the Battle of Pavia in 1525. Although the French lost the battle to the Spanish, the soup is still going strong and is highly recommended by the locals.

Another important Romanesque building is San Pietro in Ciel d'Oro; its ceiling – which was formerly gold – is mentioned in Dante's *Divine Comedy*. Lombard king Luitprand had the bones of St Augustine buried here in the year 725.

North of the town is the 14th-century Castello dei Visconti, now home to the municipal museum; to the south is the Ponte Vecchio, a covered bridge across the Ticino River (1354, restored) is also worth a detour.

CERTOSA DI PAVIA

The ★★ **Certosa di Pavia** (open Tues–Sun 9–11.30am and 2.30–4.30pm; 6pm in summer, 4pm in winter; a monk conducts tours of the building; a small tip is expected), a former Carthusian monastery, is situated roughly 27km (17 miles) to the south of Milan. It can be reached along the N35, which follows the course of the Naviglio Pavese; turn off this road 9km (6 miles) beyond Binasco (infamously, Filippo Maria Visconti had his wife Beatrice murdered in the castle here in 1418).

The monastery was founded in 1396 by Gian Galeazzo Visconti and is one of the most important architectural and cultural monuments in Italy. It was originally designed as a mausoleum for the Visconti family. The first architect was Bernardo

Old houses, Pavia

da Venezia, who was followed by Cristoforo da Cingo and Giacomo da Campione. In 1420 Giovanni Solari also worked here, and his son Guiniforte in 1453. The magnificent, almost overly ornate 15th-century façade is by Giovanni Antonio Amadeo, who was assisted by Milanese goldsmith-sculptors Cristoforo and Antonio Mantegazza between 1464 and 1495; it is considered to be the finest example of the Lombard style in existence. During the 16th century the building was finally completed in the Renaissance style.

COLLECTION HIGHLIGHTS

The monastery contains several superb pieces of sculpture, impressive wood carvings, bronzes and wrought-iron grilles, marble mosaics, intarsia, stained-glass windows and several very valuable paintings. Highlights inside the building include the 15th-century tomb of Lodovico il Moro and his wife Beatrice d'Este in the left transept, by Cristoforo Solari. The second chapel in the left side-aisle contains a 15th-century polyptych by Perugino and Bergognone. The triptych made of hippopotamus tusk with 66 bas-reliefs and 94 statuettes – all on display in the old sacristy – is from the workshop of Baldassare degli Embriachi and is Venetian (1400–1409).

Also of interest in the monastery are the high altar, the 15th-century choir-stalls and the ceiling decoration in the so-called 'new' sacristy by Pietro Solari (1600). In the right transept also note the entrance-gate to the Fountain Chapel with the busts of the seven duchesses of Milan, sculpted during the 15th century.

The **Little Cloister** is a pleasant, covered walkway built by Rinaldo de Stauris from Cremona and with delightful terracotta decoration, dating to *circa* 1465. The 122 arches of the Great Cloister are supported by marble columns; the 24 little rooms belonging to the monks seem rather too cosy, and no longer resemble proper cells. François I of France was held captive in the rooms adjoining the Great Cloister after the Battle of Pavia in 1525.

Star Attraction
● **Certosa di Pavia**

Below and bottom: scenes from the Certosa di Pavia

Map on page 88

Mussolini's murder

From Como, continue along the western bank of the lake, via Argegno, towards Tremezzo and the village of Mezzegra, where Mussolini was shot dead on 27 April 1945. He and his mistress, Claretta Petacci, were taken to Milan on the day after their execution, and their dead bodies were strung up for all to see in Piazzale Loreto. From Mezzegra, just before Cadenabbia, you will reach Villa Carlotta, built in 1747 and renowned for its garden.

Northern Italian Lakes

The French 19th-century novelist Alexandre Dumas wrote, 'What can one say about Lake Maggiore, about the Borromean Isles, about Lake Como, unless it be that one pities those that are not madly in love with them.' Since their heyday in the 19th century, when the Grand Tourists would pass through on their indulgent travels, the lakes have inspired writers such as Byron, Shelley, Stendhal, Nietszche, Goethe and Thomas Mann. Nowadays, tourists and the Italians still flock here – the fresh air and inspiring mountain views at the lakes provide the perfect complement to the rather more hectic cultural and financial opportunities available in Milan.

LAGO DI COMO

Just 156km (97 miles) and an easy day-trip by car or train from Milan, is ★ **Lago di Como** (Lake Como). If you strike lucky with the weather, the combination of glorious blue skies, the twinkling reflection of the sun on the water and the vast, snow-topped mountains around the lake will prove irresistible. Stars including Greta Garbo and Gianni Versace have had homes here – after Versace was murdered in 1998, his family scattered his ashes in the grounds of his Montrasio villa near Como.

Views across Lake Como north to the Alps

At 410m (1,345ft) Lake Como is the deepest inland lake in Europe. It measures 150sq km (58sq miles), is 50km (30 miles) long and 4.5km (2½ miles wide). Elegant villas and gardens line its banks, while it is enclosed by mountains between 1,500m (4,900ft) and 2,100m (6,890ft) in height. The southern part divides into a western and an eastern half (Lago di Lecco).

Visitors can queue to take pedalos on to the water – it's worth the wait and the rather inflated cost to escape to the relative tranquillity of the far edges of the lake and gain stunning views of the surrounding mountains. Just watch out for the sluggish steamers that pass through the lake as you pedal.

Below: yachts on the waterfront, Como
Bottom: turtles, Villa Carlotta

On the edge of the lake in the Giardino Pubblico is the **Mausoleo Voltiano** (Voltiano temple), erected to commemorate the physicist Alessandro Volta, who was born here (1745–1827) and after whom the electrical unit volt is named.

COMO

Adjacent to the lake is the town of ★ **Como**, situated 200m (660ft) above sea-level and with a population of around 95,000. The town is a centre of the silk industry and a holiday hot spot – it can become unbearably busy during the peak season or on hot weekends. For information, visit the tourist office, or APT, Piazza Cavour 17, tel: 031-3300111.

Notable sights in Como include the **Duomo**, which shows the transition from the Gothic to Renaissance architectural styles. It was finally completed by Turin architect Juvara in the 18th century with the addition of a 75-m (245-ft) high dome.

Other highlights in the town include the **Broletto** (Old Town Hall), built in 1215 in the Gothic style and notable for its elegant triple-arched windows. The **Porta Vittoria**, a gate in the city wall just south of the Duomo on Via Giove, dates mostly from the 12th century but still contains remains of the 2nd-century Porta Romana. The **Basilica San Fedele**, built mostly in the 12th century but still with its 11th-century portal sculpture, is a fine example of the Lombard Romanesque style *(see page 103).*

Map on page 88

Borromean Islands
From Stresa you can catch a boat to one of the islands known as the Isole Borromee, after the family who took possession of them in the 16th century. They are: the Isola Bella (Beautiful Island); Isola dei Pescatori (Fishermen's Island) and Isola Madre (Mother Island).

Hotel du Lac, Varenna

LECCO

An industrial and commercial centre, **Lecco** (215m/700ft above sea-level; population 46,000), is also a popular excursion destination from Milan. The remains of the 14th-century fortifications are fascinating, and a visit to the town's Duomo and Palazzo del Caleotto (where Alessandro Manzoni used to live) is rewarding. Lecco is the starting-point for trips up to the Pizzo d'Erna (1,375m/ 4,500ft) and Monte Coltignone (1,775m/5,820ft). From Lecco, you can return to Milan via the *super-strada* motorway (315km/195 miles).

VARENNA

Picturesquely situated on the east bank of Lake Como, the attractive town of **Varenna** (220m/ 720ft above sea-level; population 4,500) is a popular day trip from Milan at a distance of around 240km (150) miles. The town's narrow streets, which fall steeply down to the lake, are enlivened with elegant houses in all colours of the rainbow. Above the town (345m/1,135ft) is the ruin of the Castello di Vezio, believed to have been built for Queen Theodolinda *(see page 92)*. There are car ferry connections from here to Bellagio, where there are some fine gardens and villas.

MENAGGIO

Menaggio (203m/666ft above sea-level; population around 4,500), 191km (120 miles) from Milan, is a picturesque and much-visited little resort built on a promontory. The town has a ruined castle and offers visitors spectacular views of Bellagio at the tip of the peninsula.

LAGO DI VARESE

This lake (Lake Varese) is particularly popular among the Milanese. The town of **Varese** (382m/1,253ft above sea-level; population 84,000), is 130km (80) miles from Milan and has several places worthy of a visit. The church of San Vittore, built by Giuseppe Bernascone between 1580 and 1615 according to designs by Tibaldi, features a 70-m (235-ft) high campanile erected during the 17th and 18th centuries. Beyond the church is a 12th-century Romanesque baptistry. A walk through the Giardini Pubblici (Public Gardens), around Villa Mirabello, is delightful. Rewarding excursion destinations near here include the Sacro Monte (880m/2,880ft) and the Campo dei Fiori (1,226m/4,022ft); both offer great views.

Below and bottom:
Varenna's waterfront

LAGO DI MAGGIORE

The shortest connection between Milan and **Lago di Maggiore** (Lake Maggiore) is via the Autostrada dei Laghi, which leads to Sesto Calende – a distance of about 55km (35 miles). Lake Maggiore is around 210sq km (80sq miles) in size and 370m (1,200ft) deep, making it the largest lake in Italy after the Lago di Garda (Lake Garda). The Ticino River flows through it, and its northern end is part of Switzerland.

On the western bank of the lake is **Stresa** (210m/690ft above sea-level; population 5,000), some 80km (50 miles) from Milan and one of the most elegant tourist destinations in this part of Italy. From here take an excursion to Monte Mottarone (1,490m/ 4,890ft; cable-car), which has a good road leading up it; at the top you can enjoy superb views across the Alps.

Map
on page
88

👁 Bucket ride
For a trip with a difference take the two seater yellow 'bucket' *(funivia)* which transports you from Laveno up to Sasso di Ferro (the Rock of Iron), just behind the town, for spectacular views over the lake. Although it may seem rather perilous the gate is fixed securely, but it is a dramatic experience nonetheless. Open daily in summer and weekends in winter.

*Alpine scenery,
Lago di Maggiore*

ROCCA DI ANGERA

Angera (pop. 5,500), at the southern tip of the lake, is a busy town situated in a pretty bay opposite Arona. The main highlight here is easily spotted: the ★ **Rocca di Angera** (open Apr–Oct: 9.30am–12.30pm and 2–6pm; July and Aug 9.30am–12.30pm and 3–7pm), a proud fortress up on a hill behind the town, with a commanding view across the countryside and the lake.

The site is steeped in history; not far from the fortress is the cave known as the **Antro di Mitra**, where traces of the Mithraic cult (1st and 2nd centuries AD) were discovered. The castle dates back to the Torriani and the Visconti (14th century), and there are some fine ★ frescoes (1314) in the Gothic Sala della Giustizia depicting a Visconti victory. From the tower the view across to the Sacro Monte near Varese *(see page 98)* and the small island of Partegora is impressive.

The Rocca di Angera is now also home to the fascinating Museo della Bambola or Doll Museum (open Easter–Oct: daily 9.30am–12.30pm and 3–7pm). This is one Europe's best doll collections, and other rooms contain children's clothes from the 17th century to the present.

SANTA CATERINA DEL SASSO

Along the eastern shore of the lake, not far from the tiny village of **Reno**, is ★★ **Santa Caterina del Sasso** (open Easter–Oct: daily 8.30am–noon and 2.30–6pm; Nov–Easter 8.30am–noon and 2–5pm). A 12th-century chapel on the site became a small Dominican monastery, which was spared destruction in the 17th century when a landslide stopped within feet of the church. The site immediately became a place of pilgrimage. However, 270 years later, in 1910, another landslide smashed through the church roof, fortunately harming no one.

The church and the small monastery are at their most impressive when viewed from the lake. Inside, prized frescoes include the 16th century Danse Macabre in the convent's loggia. Access is by boat from April to September or by road – but steep steps still need to be negotiated.

LAVENO

From **Laveno** (pop. 9,000) there's a good view across the Gulf of Borromeo towards the peaks of the Valais Alps. The town itself is industrial, but the local ceramic trade has a long history. In Cerro, which is situated 3km/2 miles out of Laveno, the Civica Raccolta di Terraglia museum (open Sept–June: Tues–Thur 2.30–5.30pm, Fri–Sun 10am–noon and 2.30–5.30pm; July–Aug: Tues–Thur 3.30–6.30pm, Fri–Sun 10am–noon and 3.30–6.30pm; closed Mon) documents the development of this craft, introduced to the region in 1856.

Beyond Laveno, up towards Switzerland, is the 'Alpine' part of the eastern shore: here, the terrain becomes steeper, and the narrow road starts going through several tunnels. Soon Castelveccana comes into view, along with the famous steep rock known as the **Rocca di Caldè** (373m/1,220ft). Although a castle once stood on top of the rock, it was razed by Confederation troops in 1513.

Situated just before **Porto Valtravaglia** (pop. 2,500), which lies right beside the lake, there's an interesting alternative route (with good views) via the villages of Nasca, Musadino and Muceno to **Brezzo di Bedero**. Brezza's 12th-century church of San Vittore still retains several of its Romanesque features.

Star Attraction
● **Santa Caterina del Sasso**

Below and bottom:
Santa Caterina del Sasso

Architecture

ROMAN TIMES TO THE MIDDLE AGES

The earliest remaining examples of Milanese architecture date back to when the city was a Roman settlement. To the southwest of the city centre are the ruins of a huge Roman circus and the Colonne di San Lorenzo, columns of a building erected in the 2nd or 3rd century AD. The octagonal church of San Lorenzo dates from the 4th century and is in the squat architectural style that is typical of the early Christian period.

Through the ages, Milan's importance as a religious centre has been reflected in its proliferation of churches. In the Middle Ages the Lombard Romanesque dominated *(see box, right)*. By the mid-13th century the influence of the Gothic style was appearing in Lombardy. The Lombard builders were not keen on the upwards-striving forms typical of the French Gothic, preferring instead classical horizontal lines and broad interior spaces. Even Milan Cathedral (begun 1386), which could be said to be the most strongly Gothic church in Italy and certainly recalls the French style in many of its features, also evinces a great deal of influence from the Northern Italian tradition. In other Gothic Milanese churches, such as San Marco (1254) and San Gottardo (1336), the Lombard rearrangement of the Gothic is evident, as it is in the magnificent Gothic cathedral of Como, which was built between the 14th and 16th centuries.

THE RENAISSANCE

By the start of the 15th century builders in Florence were moving away from the Gothic in favour of a renaissance of classical designs and motifs. Rounded arches, classical columns and emphasis on the horizontal, achieved, for example, by cornices, are all characteristic of Renaissance architecture. However, it wasn't until 1456 that architecture in the early Renaissance style was seen as far north as Milan. Despite fierce resistance from the Lombard artists and architects

Lombard Romanesque
Churches in this style are characteristically dark but clearly proportioned with richly decorated portals and porches, and square bell towers. The oldest churches of this type in Milan are San Celso (10th century) and San Babila (11th century), while Sant'Ambrogio (4th–12th century) and San Simpliciano (12th century) are the most stylistically pure. Como's San Fidele and Bergamo's Santa Maria Maggiore (both 12th century) are Lombard Romanesque.

Opposite: the Colonne di San Lorenzo, Milan
Below: Santa Maria Maggiore, Bergamo

Antonio Sant'Elia
This architect (1888–1916) is generally considered to be the father of Italian Futurism, a style that emerged in the early 20th century and was based on the vision of cities as futuristic metropolises, dominated by soaring skycrapers, cleverly managed, multi-level traffic systems and industrial buildings designed with both appearance and purpose in mind. Tragically, Sant'Elia was killed in World War I before any of his designs were realised.

Castello Sforzesco

who wanted to retain the pointed arch, the Florentine Antonio Averulino, known as Filarete, built the Ospedale Maggiore and the gate tower of the Castello Sforzesco. The Renaissance in Milan developed with Sant' Eustorgio's Cappella Portinari *(see page 86)*, by Florentine architect Michelozzo Michelozzi.

The climax of Renaissance architecture in Milan is represented in the creations of Donato Bramante (1444–1514), who worked in the city for Lodovico il Moro from 1480 to 1499 and produced the choir and dome of Santa Maria delle Grazie and the baptistry of San Satiro. Bramante's influence is evident in the buildings of the architect family Solari, especially Cristoforo Solari (called Il Gobbo, died 1525). The façade of the Carthusian monastery in Pavia *(see page 94)* by Giovanni Antonio Amadeo (1447–1522) and his Cappella Colleoni in Bergamo are also important examples of Lombard Renaissance style.

The greatest exponent of the Late Renaissance in Milan is the Perugian Galeazzo Alessi (1512–72), who designed Piazza alla Scala's imposing Palazzo Marino. The work of the Bolognese master Pellegrino Tibaldi (1532–96) in the courtyard of the archbishop's palace already mark a transition to early baroque.

THE BAROQUE TO THE 19TH CENTURY

Of the baroque masters of the 17th century working in Milan, Lorenzo Binaghi and Francesco Maria Richini (Palazzo Brera and the former Ospedale Maggiore) are the most notable. Exponents of neoclassicism, a style that grew as a reaction to the excesses of the baroque and is characterised by a return to clean, solid lines and minimal decoration, include Giuseppe Piermarini (1734–1808), with numerous buildings including the Teatro alla Scala and the Palazzo Reale.

The late 18th and early 19th centuries were typically turbulent times for the Milanese. In 1786 Napoleon made Milan the capital of his new Italian state, and his architectural legacy includes two grand gates befitting an emperor: the Porta

Ticinese, designed by Luigi Cagnola, and Porta Venezia, by Ridolfo Vantini. Further new structures were planned, but Napoleon's days were numbered, and by 1814 the Austrians were back in charge of Milan.

After the unification of Italy in 1861, Milan's status as Italy's most important centre of business, finance and industry became ever more assured – something that has been reflected in its architecture from that point on. Perhaps the greatest building of the 19th century in Milan is the magnificent Galleria Vittorio Emanuele II *(see page 22),* designed by Giuseppe Mengoni and revolutionary in the city (although not internationally) for its glass and iron construction.

THE 20TH CENTURY AND BEYOND

The first ground-breaking style of the turn of the 20th century, art nouveau, representing a return to forms and motifs inspired by nature, is evident in Milan in buildings such as Palazzo Castiglioni. In between the wars, Milanese architecture was subject to the tastes of the ruling Fascists – the heavy form of Milan's Stazione Centrale is a fine example of this. In the immediate post-war years, architectural efforts were concentrated on rapid housing projects, as the city had been badly bombed. In more stylish terms,

Below: Stazione Centrale fascist architecture
Bottom: Milanese lion

the Grattacielo Pirelli (or 'Pirello' – Big Pirelli – as it is popularly known), built 1955–60 to designs by Giò Ponti, among others, succeeded in realising the vision of Sant'Elia *(see box on page 104)*; until the end of the 1960s, this skyscraper was the tallest in the world), as did Studio BBPR's medieval-inspired, top-heavy Torre Velasca *(see page 76)*, erected in 1958. Less notable blocks – with which the city is often perhaps unfairly exclusively connected – also sprang up at this time. Most recent examples of notable architecture include Marco Zanuso's Nuovo Piccolo (now known as the Teatro Strehler after the influential Milanese theatre director who spearheaded the project) and Teatro Studio, also part of the Strehler legacy.

Below: Milanese portrait
Bottom: Leonardo drawing

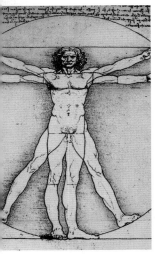

Sculpture

Lombard sculpture developed slowly, lagging behind that of the rest of Italy until the 14th century. The first major impulses were provided by the great tomb sculptures of Giovanni di Balduccio, who came to Milan from Pisa and worked here between 1321 and 1339. However, it was the influence of Florentine Renaissance that led to the blossoming *circa* 1460 of a Lombard sculptural school that was to have an enormous impact on developments across Italy. The principal exponents of the art were Cristoforo Mantegazza (died 1482), Giovanni Antonio Amadeo, Cristoforo Solari and Tommaso Rodari (1487–1533). High Renaissance masters included Cristoforo Foppa (called Caradosso, 1445–1527) who was also a renowned goldsmith, and Agostino Busti (called Bambaia, 1480–1548), whose works mark the end of the development of Lombard sculpture.

Painting

Heading the list of important painters working in Lombardy is Vincenzo Foppa (died 1515), who trained in Padua and displayed a strongly traditional approach. Foppa was followed by his poetically inclined student Ambrogio da Fossano, called Borgognone (died 1523). Influenced initially by Vincenzo Foppa and then by Bramante, the Milanese Bartolomeo Suardi, called Bramantino (1455–1536), possessed a changing sense of style.

The high point of Renaissance painting in Milan is undoubtedly marked by the works of Leonardo da Vinci (1452–1519), who lived and worked in the city between 1482–1500 and 1506–8. Among his closest students were Giovanni Boltraffio (1467–1516), Marco D'Oggionó (1470–1530), Cesare da Sesto (died in 1521), Andrea Salaino (1470–1515), Giampietrino (active 1508–21), and, most lauded, Bernardino Luini (1470–1530). Gaudenzio Ferrari (1471– 1546) and his student Bernardino Lanino (died 1578) are two of the finest Lombard Renaissance painters. The principal exponent of neoclassicism in the area is Andrea Appiani (1754–1817), while the 19th century is best represented by the works of Francesco Hayez (1754–1815), former director of the Brera and especially noted for *The Kiss*, now displayed at the Pinacoteca *(see page 43)*.

Milanese writers
One of the most important Italian poets of the 18th century was Milan resident Giuseppe Parini (1729–99), whose elegant satires were later taken up by Carlo Porta (1775–1821) in his dialect poetry. Among the notable 19th-century Italian Romantic authors from the region, Milan-born Alessandro Manzoni (1785–1873) is famous for his historical novels such as *The Betrothed*, a novel set in 17th-century Milan.

Music

Of immense importance for the development of European music as a whole was the introduction of hymns in church by the Milanese archbishop

Piazza della Scala, 1880

Opera etiquette
Brave visitors who wish to show their appreciation can shout *bravo* for tenors, *brava* for sopranos and *bravi* to congratulate everyone. Ultimately, as long as the opera provides a spectacle, of people-watching or, perish the thought, of mellifluous music, then an Italian audience usually goes home happy, whether the fat lady sings or not.

St Ambrose (339–397). Since the 18th century the development of opera has been closely linked with the Teatro alla Scala *(see page 28)*, generally considered to be one of the greatest opera houses in the world. Gaetano Donizetti (1797–1848), Gioacchino Rossini (1792–1868), Vincenzo Bellini (1801–35), Giuseppe Verdi (1813–1901), Arturo Toscanini (1867–1957) and Maria Callas (1923–77) are just some of the great operatic stars associated with La Scala.

Musicians who have made their mark here recently include the pianist Maurizio Pollini and conductors Riccardo Chailly, Claudio Abbado and Riccardo Muti. The internationally renowned modernist composer, Luciano Berio, who experiments with sound in all its forms, from electronic and rock music to folk, jazz and classical, was honoured at La Scala prior to its closure for restoration, with a premiere of his opera *Outis*.

Self-portrait by Donizetti

Nightlife

MUSIC

As described above, the **Teatro alla Scala**, famed for its wonderful acoustics, glittering performers, and equally sumptuous interiors, is Milan's main venue for opera. Note that while the main house is closed for restoration (until 2004), performances are being held at the Teatro degli Arcimbaldi *(see page 29)*. A programme of concerts runs from June to mid-July and from October until November.

Most other classical concerts are held in churches across Milan. Main venues include: **San Marco** (Piazza San Marco 2) for religious music; the **Civica Scuola di Musica** (Via Stilicone 36) for more contemporary music; the **Conservatorio Giuseppe Verdi** (Via Conservatorio 12), a former monastery where concerts by various orchestras are held almost daily; the **Musica e Poesia a San Maurizio** (San Maurizio, on the Corso Magenta) for ancient and baroque music; **Santa Maria del Carmine** (Piazza del Carmine 2), which stages regular concerts, from chamber music to Gregorian chant; and **Teatro delle Erbe** (Via Mercato 3) for classical and guitar works. Rock music concerts take place at **Palavobis** (Metro: Lampugnano) or at **Filaforum di Assago** (Metro: Romolo, then shuttle bus).

THEATRE AND FILM

Milan has a lively theatre scene with numerous permanent theatres and independent groups. If you think your knowledge of the Italian language is too rudimentary to follow a major performance, you might still enjoy a visit to a fringe piece at the **Piccolo Teatro di Milano** (Via Rovello 2) founded by Milanese theatre giant, the late director Giorgio Strehler (1921–97) or the **Teatro Strehler** (formerly known as the Nuovo Piccolo, Largo Greppi). At the **Teatro Franco Parenti** (Via Pier Lombardo 14), plays and concerts, including musicals for children, are staged.

For film buffs, there are over 100 cinemas across Milan, with most of the big screens grouped around Corso Vittorio Emanuele II. The majority of films shown in Milan are dubbed – if you want to see a work in its original language, look for 'VO' (for *versione originale)* in the programme. Numerous film festivals are held throughout the year; for details of what's on when, consult the useful free bulletin *Milano Mese*.

Below: art nouveau hotel
Bottom: the Brera

FOOD AND DRINK

Strictly speaking, Italian cuisine as such doesn't actually exist; instead there are a host of regional variations. Luckily, in Milan it is possible to sample not only the local Milanese specialities but those from elsewhere in the country as well. Although Milan is an expensive city, food prices are surprisingly reasonable and you can eat out very well here on a modest budget.

BREAKFAST

The first meal of the day in Milan tends to be a light affair, typically consisting of a *cornetto* (pastry) or croissant washed down with a *cappuccino* or *latte*. For some Milanese, breakfast is little more than a short, strong *espresso,* just enough to kick start the day. If you breakfast at one of the city's bars or cafés, you'll be charged more for sitting at a table than for standing at the counter. In some traditional bars and cafés, you need to collect a voucher *(scontrino)* for what you want from the cashier before ordering; in a growing number of cafés, however, you simply order, eat and then ask for a bill before you leave.

LUNCH

Across much of Italy, especially the South, lunch *(pranzo)* has traditionally been the main meal of the day. However, in the industrialised north, especially in such business-orientated cities as Milan, that tradition is being squeezed out in favour of short, employer-friendly lunch breaks. Milan has more than its fair share of pizzerias, grills, *Tavola Calde* (hot tables) and *paninoteche,* which serve light, rapidly prepared lunches or food that can be consumed on the hoof. If you've got time to sit and relax, don't judge a restaurant by its exterior – often the best food is available at the most modest-looking establishment.

DINNER

With lunch no longer the main meal of the day in Milan, dinner is generally the most lavish meal, consisting of several courses. Prior to dinner, it is customary to have an *aperitif,* of which there are countless types, from alcohol-free versions *(bitter analcolico)* to orange-flavoured Campari. Italians usually eat at least two or three courses for dinner: a starter such as *prosciutto* and melon, followed by a pasta or rice dish *(risotto)* as a first course *(primo),* then a second course *(secondo)* of meat or fish, accompanied by vegetables or salad (for a range of popular dishes and Milanese specialities, *see next page).* If you still have room, this can all be followed by one of many mouth-watering desserts *(dolce),* cheese *(formaggio)* or fruit *(frutta).* If you don't think you can manage such a vast amount of food, just eat as many courses as you want to. Restaurant owners are usually quite relaxed about this.

Italians often round off their meals with an *espresso*, sometimes laced

Risotto alla Milanese
The recipe below, for this ultimate Milanese dish, is true to the original and serves four people. First, soak 20g (½oz) dried mushrooms in lukewarm water. Next, finely chop a small onion and fry it gently in 30g (1oz) of butter. Add either 30g (1oz) of beef marrow or 2 teaspoons of dripping – beef marrow is more traditional – and stir well. Now, take 8 or 9 handfuls of rice and add them to the frying onions; stir well and cook the rice briefly, so that it glistens. Add the rehydrated mushrooms and, gradually, 1 litre (2 pints) of stock. When the rice is cooked, add a pinch of saffron to colour the dish, stir in a generous portion of grated Parmesan and a little more butter, mix well and serve.

with a dash of *grappa* or brandy *(caffè corretto)*. An alternative is to drink a digestif *(un amaro)* such as *grappa*, *amaretto* or, a local speciality, the spicy, herby Ramazzotti.

DRINKS

Apart from the *digestifs* and *aperitifs* mentioned above, wine is the most popular option to accompany a meal. Local wines *(vino locale)* are much better value than those from further afield, and you'll find that the Italians are very keen on promoting their own wines – hence a distinct lack of varieties from other countries on many wine lists. Good local whites in Milan include: Franciacorta Pinot, Lugana, Tocai di Lugana, Trebbiano, Riesling and Cortese. Notable reds include: Sassella, Grumello, Inferno, Valgella, Cellatica, Botticino, Riviera del Garda, and Quistellese. Beer is available in all restaurants but tends to be rather expensive. Mineral water *(acqua minerale)* is popular and is available fizzy *(gasata)* or non-fizzy *(naturale)*.

Milanese specialities

Lombard cooking tends to be quality, fuss-free, filling fare. Many Milanese dishes are cooked slowly, with stews and *risottos* dominating the menu. Some Milanese specialities – those made with veal, tripe and pig's trotters, for example – may not be for the squeamish, but much of the local fare is well worth tasting. Pescivores are well catered for with fish and seafood dishes, while pure vegetarians should find a reasonable number of salads plus egg, cheese and vegetable dishes on the menu.

FIRST COURSES AND SOUPS

Among the first-course dishes, *primi*, is the main city dish, *risotto alla Milanese* – rice cooked in saffron and stock *(see recipe on previous page)*, also known as *risotto con lo zafferano* (saffron risotto). According to popular belief, in the 16th century a young glazier called Zafferano (Saffron) coloured his glazes for the windows of the Duomo with his spice namesake; on his wedding day he likewise 'gilded' a risotto he made for his new bride. All manner of pastas are also offered as *primi*.

A typical Milanese soup is *busecca* – tripe soup with chopped parsley or beans. *Minestrone alla milanese* is a kind of vegetable soup, which is eaten hot in winter, and either hot or cold in summer, while the equivalent from nearby Pavia, *zuppa pavese*, is a hot meat soup, usually served with toasted bread, egg and grated cheese.

SECOND COURSES

Among the *secondi* on the local menu, you'll find *bresàola* – dried and smoked fillet of beef, eaten either cold (marinated in oil and lemon juice) or hot, fried with parsley, garlic, onions and herbs. *Cassoeula* is a stew made with pork, pig's trotters, sausage and cabbage. Another popular dish, *costoletta alla milanese*, is a breaded escalope of veal, similar to a *Wiener Schnitzel*, while *ossobuco* is a leg of veal cut into thin slices, cooked lightly with bone marrow and tomato purée and served with *risotto*, mashed potato or *polenta*. *Stufato* is a beef pot roast heavily flavoured with herbs and spices.

DESSERTS AND CHEESES

Puddings tend to be light, with ice-creams and sorbets dominating the sweet menu. Fruit is also popular. *Panettone*, a sponge cake, typically eaten at Christmas, comes from Milan. Cheeses you'll find on the menu include Gorgonzola, Mascarpone, Stracchino, Grana (similar to Parmesan), Robiola, Taleggio, Fontina and Bel Paese.

Eating Out

Following is a selection of bars, cafés and restaurants, in alphabetical order. Many restaurants close at least one day in the week and perhaps also during August, so it's advisable to check they're open in advance. Prices, which are quoted as guides only, are for dinner for one, excluding wine. Note that a cover charge *(coperto)* will often be added to the bill, and an extra service charge may also be added.

€€€: around 50 euros
€€: around 30 euros
€: around 15 euros

Al Girarrosto di Cesarino, Corso Venezia 31, tel: 02-76000481. For a change from the ubiquitous Milanese stews and *risottos*, try traditional Tuscan cuisine, served here in an elegant setting. **€€**

Al Mercante, Piazza Mercante 17, tel: 02-805 2198. Quality reliable Italian cuisine in an atmospheric medieval courtyard, just a stone's throw from the Duomo. **€€**

Armani/Nobu, Via Pisoni 1, tel: 02-62312645. Modern, minimalist ambience at Emporio Armani. Original and innovative cuisine. On the ground floor there is a sushi bar, while upstairs the restaurant offers fusion food combining the flavours of Japan with South America and the West. Open: evenings only on Sat and Mon, lunch only Tues–Fri. **€€€**

Bar Brera, Via Brera 23, tel: 02-877 091. Located on the corner of the bohemian Brera's main thoroughfare, right opposite the Pinacoteca di Brera, this café offers value-for-money lunches, from tasty hot *panini* to big bowls of pasta. There are lots of tables outside, which are heated in winter. Good place for a coffee. **€**

Biffi Scala Toula, Piazza Scala, tel: 02-866651. This restaurant prepares stylish twists on classic gourmet cuisine plus some Venetian dishes. Great location next to La Scala and the Galleria Vittorio Emanuele II. **€€€**

Bistrot Duomo, Via San Raffaele 2, tel: 02-877 120. Offset the pricey menu with the splendid views over the Duomo's lofty spires at this restaurant on the top floor of La Rinascente department store. The plexiglass roof comes off in summer. Lovely in the evenings. **€€€**

Boeucc, Piazza Belgioioso 2 , tel: 02-76020224. Here, traditional Lombard fare, such as veal dishes and risottos, are served in the grand, frescoed

Popular eating places in the trendy canal quarter

Belgioioso Palazzo. Formal dress is the order of the day – jackets for men at lunchtime, suits in the evening. A city institution. €€€

Caffè Letterario, Via Solferino 27, tel: 02-2901 5119. This cool café is a great place to go for a quiet read or simply to while away the hours. Popular with Milan's intellegentsia. €

Caajunco, Via Stoppani 5, tel: 02-2046003. Pescivores and other fish-lovers should enjoy the range of Sicilian seafood here. €€

Capolinea, Via Ludovico Il Moro 119, tel: 02-89122024. Dine late in this fashionable jazz and blues club/restaurant, well located in the trendy canal quarter. €€

Don Carlos, Grand Hotel et de Milan, Via Manzoni 29, tel: 02-723141. A Milanese institution in the city's most historic hotel, this restaurant is popular for late dining. Does subtle classic Italian dishes as well as Milanese specialities. Dress smartly. €€€

El Brellin, Vicolo Lavandai, off Alzaia Naviglio Grande, tel: 02-58101351. At this converted mill in the canal quarter, Milanese dishes are served to the sound of a live pianist. The restaurant's traditional setting is counterbalanced by a decidedly hip clientele. €€

Il Fondaco dei Mori, Via Solferino 33, tel: 02-653711. Tucked into a *palazzo* in the Brera, this fashionable Somali restaurant offers dishes from all over the Arab world. It's worth paying the extra for the tented Berber corner, where dishes are served among cushions and tribal rugs. €€

Il Luogo di Aimo e Nadia, Via Montecuccoli 6, tel: 02-416886. A temple to gastronomy, this place is acclaimed as one of Italy's top restaurants. Some Tuscan influence characterises the deceptively simple but superbly executed dishes. Reservations are essential. €€€

Il Teatro, Four Seasons Hotel, Via Gesù 8, tel: 02-77081435. Creative, sophisticated, light cuisine is offered in a former convent at the heart of the fashion district. Note that the restaurant is open for dinner only. €€€

Joia, Via Castaldi 18, tel: 02-29522124. One for the vegetarians, Joia offers top-class meat-free food, and separate rooms for smokers and non-smokers. €€

La Bella Pisana, Via Sottocorno 17, tel: 02-76021803. Come here for Padana plain cooking, fresh fish and a pleasant ambience. The garden is open in summer. Reserve. €€

La Dolce Vita, Via Bergamini 11, tel: 02-583303843. A romantic and highly sophisticated spot with candles and coffered ceilings, and a kitchen that stays open until midnight. Lombard specialities, *nouvelle cuisine* and gourmet menus (less pricey at lunchtime). €€€

La Scaletta, Piazzale Stazione di Porta Genova, tel: 02-58100290. Come to this fashionable canal quarter restaurant for fine seafood, good risottos and great homemade pasta and bread. The restaurant is decorated with modern art and even has a library. It's popular, so reserve. Open evenings only. €€€

La Tana del Lupo, Viale Vittorio Veneto 30, tel: 02-6599006. Venetian cuisine is dished up in a cosy setting, often to the strains of a live harmonica. €

Malastrana, Ripa di Porta Ticinese 65, tel: 02-8378984. Another canal district pizzaria with a courtyard – this one is especially good for late dining. It's smaller than El Brellin *(see above)* but even more authentic. €

Orient Express, Via Fiori Chiari 8, tel: 02-8056227. The Orient Exress is a chic theme bar and restaurant in the style of the famous train. Live piano music. Also serves brunch. €€€

Peck, Via Victor Hugo 4, tel: 02-876774. At this distinguished temple of gastronomy, updated Italian cuisine is served in an elegant, modern setting, and the service is second to none. If the prices here are too high, visit the wonderful delicatessen/tearoom of the same name in Via Spadari 9 instead. €€€

Premiata Pizza, Alzaia Naviglio Grande 2, tel: 02-894 0648. Premiata Pizza is an inexpensive pizzeria with a pleasant courtyard in the lively canal district. €

Radetzky, Largo La Foppa 5, tel: 02-657 2645. Despite its ultra-hip interior the urban Radetzky is unintimidating and is a fabulous place for morning coffee and evening cocktails alike. There's a big round table – good for making friends – or, for the more private among you, there are smaller tables by the windows. €–€€

Ristorante Solferino, Via Castelfidardo 2, tel: 02-29005748. Just next door to the highly recommended Antica Locanda Solferino hotel (*see page 125*) is this gorgeous restaurant, which is a perfect choice for a romantic candlelit dinner for two. Delicious Milanese cuisine is served in delight-

ful, old-world surroundings. Attentive staff and a great wine list promise an evening to remember. Great location in the Brera. €€

Sadler, Via Conchetta (corner of Via Troilo 14), tel: 02-58104451. Highly acclaimed creative cuisine in a modern, elegant and prestigious setting. Specialities include fish and white truffles (in season). Excellent, professional service. Open for dinner only. Closed: Sunday and for a period in January and August. Reservations essential. €€€

Sadler Wine & Food, Via Monte Bianco 2/A, tel: 02-4814677. Elegant, but informal, this is a smaller version of Sadler on Via Conchetta, with continuous opening from midday until 11pm. Innovative cuisine based on classic favourites. €€

Savini, Galleria Vittorio Emanuele II, tel: 02-72003433. A famous and elegantly decorated spot right in the city's Galleria, albeit somewhat on the stuffy side. Prices are high, owing to the prime location, but it's a grand place to enjoy a morning coffee. If your budget allows, try the classic Italian cuisine. Closed Sunday. €€€

Suntory Italia, Via Verdi 6, tel: 02-862210. Arguably the best Japanese restaurant in Milan, offering quality food, private rooms and a sophisticated atmosphere. €€€

Trattoria 23 Risotti, Piazza Carbonari 5, tel: 02-6704710. This traditional trattoria offers every type of *risotto* imaginable. €€

Trattoria Milanese, Via Santa Marta 11, tel: 02-86451991. True to its name, this is a classic trattoria. It serves carefully prepared traditional Milanese dishes such as *antipasti, nervetti* (boiled calf's head with mixed pickles), *pesciolini in carpione* (fish in batter with raisins and wine) and Lombard wines amid a lovely nostalgic atmosphere. €€

Sweet treats

If your sugar levels are low, visit one of Milan's many top-class confectioners *(pasticcerie)*. For a start, try:

Biffi, Corso Magenta 87. A *pasticcerie* selling wonderful traditional cakes.

Cova, Via Montenapoleone. A chic *pasticcerie* in the equally stylish fashion district.

Peck *(see restaurant entry, above)*.

And if the city heat is getting to you, cool down at one of Milan's ice-cream parlours *(gelaterie)*. Those in the centre of town include: **Grasso**, Via Cellini 1; **La Cremeria**, Via Dante 6; **Odeon**, Piazza Duomo 2; and **Passerini**, Via Victor Hugo 4.

SHOPPING

FASHION CENTRAL

Milan's bi-annual fashion shows have put the city firmly on the map in terms of its sartorial clout. This is designer fashion central, and all the big-name couturiers have branches here. Conveniently for shoppers – window- or otherwise – the main designers are concentrated in one area, around vias Montenapoleone, della Spiga, Sant'Andrea and Santo Spirito. In Via Montenapoleone and its side streets you'll see the names of Milan's most famous fashion designers, from **Gucci** and **Ferragamo** (Via Montenapoleone) to **Valentino** (Via San Spirito for womenswear, Via Montenapoleone for menswear) and from **Ferrè**, **Krizia** and **Versace** (Via della Spiga) to **Armani** and **Trussardi** (Via Sant'Andrea) and many more.

If your budget doesn't quite stretch to couture, there are more affordable shops and department stores around the Piazza dell Duomo. La Rinascente is the city-centre kingpin, but there are also numerous big chains and more exclusive boutiques along Corso Vittorio Emanuele II, Corso Buenos Aires, Corso di Porta Romana and Corso Vercelli. The Brera is excellent for individual boutiques, especially for stylish footwear.

> **Best for bookworms**
> Milan is the capital of the Italian book trade, and each of the big publishing houses runs its own bookshop here. Galleria Vittorio Emanuele II is home to many bookstores – Rizzoli has a large store here, with internet access available inside; art book specialist Bocca also has a branch in the Galleria. Other major publishing names represented include Feltrinelli (Via Manzoni 12) and Hoepli (Via Hoepli 5) – the latter is the largest bookshop in Italy.

FOOD AND ANTIQUES

The ultimate in Milanese gastronomy can be purchased at **Peck**, Via Torino *(see previous page)*, and **Il Salumaio**, Via Montenapoleone. Meanwhile the largest concentrations of antiques shops can be found around the arty Brera area and in the wealthy side streets off Via Montenapoleone.

MARKETS

Milan has several traditional markets, known as the *mercati all'aperto* (open markets) and *mercatini communali* (mini communal markets). These include the antiques and bric-a-brac **Fiera di Senigallia**, held all day Saturday at the Darsena di Viale d'Annunzia. On the last Sunday of the month the **Mercatone dell' Antiquariato**, an antiques-fair-cum-Milanese-folk-festival, is held along the Ripa Ticinese and the Navigli Grande. Food and household goods markets are also very popular with the Milanese, not least because of the very reasonable prices they offer. A good example of this type of market is the Saturday one, held on Viale Apiniano.

Each third Saturday of the month (except during August) the **Mercatino dell'Antiquariato** is held in the Brera's cobbled Via Fiori Chiari. Bag and jewellery sellers, typically parading fake Prada, Gucci and Louis Vuitton designs, set up ad hoc stalls here every evening to tempt locals and tourists alike.

Other markets include the **Fiera degli Oh bei, Oh bei**, a large antiques and flea market, which traditionally takes place on 7 and 8 December around the Basilica di Sant'Ambrogio. For book-lovers, there is the **Vecchi Libri in Piazza**, which is held on the third Sunday of the month, except July and August, in the Piazza Diaz.

PRACTICAL INFORMATION

Getting There

BY AIR

The nearest airport to Milan is **Linate** (10km/6 miles east of the city); however, since the lengthy refurbishment and expansion of the city's other airport, Malpensa, Linate has been used mainly for domestic Italian flights.

Malpensa (located 45km/28 miles northwest of the city), Milan's principal intercontinental airport, has two terminals and is served by several major companies including Alitalia (www.alitalia.com), British Airways (www.british-airways.com), British Midland and Lufthansa.

The airport is connected to Stazione Cadorna, Milan's second most busy railway station, by the efficient Malpensa Express train service (tel: 02-40099260), which runs roughly every 30 minutes from 5.30am to 1.30am.The journey takes around 50 minutes. An Air Pullman bus service ferries passengers between Malpensa and Milan's main railway station, Stazione Centrale. Buy your ticket for this shuttle service from the Air Pullman office. A taxi ride from Malpensa to the centre of Milan will cost around €50 one way.

If you are flying from the UK and planning to visit the Italian Lakes, another option is to fly by budget airline Ryanair (www.ryanair.com). Planes fly from London Stansted to the small airport at Brescia. This small town is situated approximately 80km (50 miles) from Milan and on the main rail line between there and Venice.

BY RAIL

If you are travelling from the UK, the most direct way is to take the Eurostar (www.eurostar.com) to the Gard du Nord in Paris, then cross to the Gare du Lyon for overnight services to Milan. Anyone arriving by train in Milan will arrive at Stazione Centrale, Stazione Cadorna, Stazione Garibaldi, Stazione Lambrate or Stazione Piazza Duca d'Aosta. Metro lines 1, 2 and 3 will then take you into the centre and Piazza del Duomo. For information on rail services within Italy, visit www.trenitalia.it

If you're leaving Milan, you must frank your ticket in the yellow ticket machine at the entrance to the platform before boarding the train; failure to do this is likely to result in a fine.

Milan is designer-label heaven

The platforms at the Stazione Centrale are up on the first floor, where you can also find Travel Information (tel: 02-72524360/70), a bank (Banca delle Comunicazioni, open Mon–Sat 8am–2pm), an automatic currency exchange, several boutiques, a 24-hour pharmacy, a self-service restaurant (open 11.30am–10pm) and a supermarket (open 7am–midnight). The tourist office (APT, open 8am–7pm) is on the same level, off the departure lounge. There's also a day hotel in the station, and a post office, on the ground floor.

BY CAR

In keeping with its importance as an economic centre, Milan is served by an extensive motorway network (A1 = *Autostrada del Sole*; A4 = *Serenissima*; A7 = *Autostrada dei Fiori*; A8 and A9 = *Autostrada dei Laghi*, as well as the ringroad *Tangenziale Ovest* and *Est*.

Visitors coming from Switzerland can approach Milan by motorway via Aosta, Sesto Calende, Chiasso and Como; those travelling from Austria can head over the Brenner Pass to Verona. There are toll charges on all motorways in Italy.

The Azienda Trasporti Municipali (ATM), the municipal transport system, has a series of supervised car parks along the major arterial roads leading into the city. Electronic sign boards give information on the nearest car parks and how many places are left. Thus anyone arriving via the motorways or major roads can park his or her car safely at the various public transport terminals (eg of the Metro system).

Vehicle-registration documents, a driving licence, a warning triangle and country stickers are compulsory. The international green insurance card doesn't have to be shown at the

Milan's one-way system

A complicated one-way system allows entry to Milan's city centre at certain points only. You can obtain a zonal map from a car-hire centre or from the tourist office. Before parking in a central blue zone you'll need a 'Sosta Milano' disc (purchased from bars or *tabacchi* kiosks displaying the ATM sign as well as selected Metro stations). Note that unlawfully parked cars will be towed away; should this happen to you, ring the police *(vigili urbani)* on 02-77271 and ask for Uffizio.

border but is advisable in case of an accident; comprehensive cover is highly recommended.

The following speed limits apply to motor traffic in Italy unless otherwise indicated: 50kph (30mph) in built-up areas, 90kph (55mph) on country roads, and 130kph (75mph) on motorways *(autostrada)*. Speed limits are often lowered at weekends or on public holidays. Police checks have become much stricter in recent times, and excessive speed as well as excessive alcohol consumption can cost motorists their licence – this also applies to foreign drivers. Seat belts are compulsory in Italy.

The number to ring in case of breakdown in Italy is: 116. The SOS emergency number is 113.

BY COACH

With the proliferation of low-cost airlines, the cost of travelling to Italy from Great Britain by scheduled coach is not much cheaper than travelling by air, and, of course, much slower. National Express Eurolines run coaches from London Victoria, via Paris and Mont Blanc, to Milan. To book from London, contact: Eurolines, 52 Grosvenor Gardens, London SW1W 0AU, tel: 020-7730 8235, www.eurolines.com

Getting Around

PUBLIC TRANSPORT

Milan is Italy's business capital and a regular player on the international design and fashion markets, with regular exhibitions at the city's Fiera and twice-yearly fashion shows held here. Thankfully, the city's slick, inexpensive and user-friendly public transport system is in line with Milan's smart international image.

Maps showing the city's public transport system can be obtained free from rail and metro stations, airports, newsagents, kiosks, the city transport office (ATM) in the Duomo Metro station and the tourist information centres in Stazione Centrale and Via Marconi 1. *See also the map of the metro on page 120.*

Buses and trams

The bus and tram service (ATM) is fast and efficient. Tickets must be purchased in advance at tobacconists *(tabacchi)* or newsstands and are valid for 75 minutes of travel.

The Metro

The **Metropolitana Milanese** (MM), the best subway in Italy, has four lines, which serve almost all the city and its hinterland. Trains run from 6am until about 12.30am Tickets are sold at machines in stations, in most *tabacchi* and at newsstands. A single ticket *(biglietto ordinario)* is valid for 75 minutes of travel and allows for one journey on the metro plus unlimited tram and bus journeys within that time frame. Day and two-day tickets, valid on all forms of transport, are also available, as are books of 10 tickets; these offer good value for money and are convenient if you plan to make several trips. Parents should note that children shorter than 1m/3ft 3in travel free on the metro.

PEDESTRIANS

Although Milan is an easy city to navigate on foot, Italian drivers are infamously fast and furious, so take great care when crossing the road. Even when the light at a pedestrian crossing is green, take an extra look around to check that no cars are coming. Parts of the city provide a pedestrian paradise, however – the zones around the Duomo and some parts of the Brera and Via Montenapoleone are car free.

TAXIS

Milan's distinctive white taxis can be hailed at any of the many designated ranks in the city – there is a list of these in the *Pagine Gialle* (Yellow Pages).

Waiting at Stazione Centrale

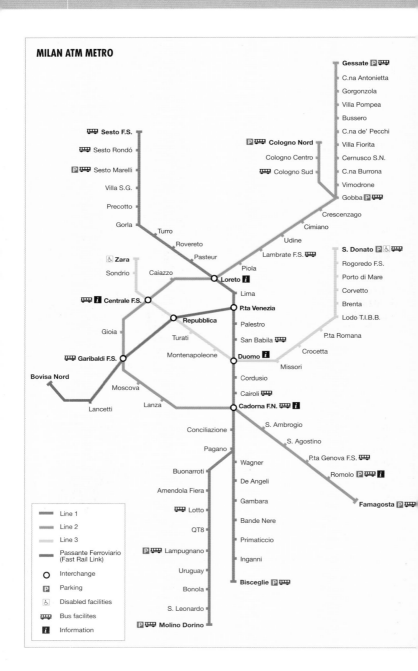

Individual cab ranks can also be contacted by phone (again, consult the phone book for their numbers). Travel by taxi tends to be relatively expensive, with a minimum charge automatically levied, plus surcharges added for extra luggage, night-time journeys (between 10pm and 7am) and travel on bank holidays. For radio-taxis, dial any one of the following:
Ambrosiana Radio Taxi: 02-5353
Arco Radio Taxi: 02-6767
Esperia Radio Taxi: 02-8383
Radio Taxi: 02-8585

HIRE CARS
These are available from Stazione Centrale and from Linate and Malpensa airports, as well as from Hertz (tel: 02-6690061), Eurodollar (tel: 02-66710104) and Avis (tel: 02-6690280), among others. Further information on car hire is available from the APT and all the major hotels.

BUS AND TRAM TOURS
From Tuesday to Sunday the travel agency Autostradale organises bus tours of Milan, which leave from in front of Palazzo Reale at the south side of the Duomo and last 3 hours, taking in all the major sights. Reservations can be made in several Milan travel agencies and at the tourist office (tel: 02-72524301/2/3).

In addition, there is a tram tour of the city, Tram Turistico (tel: 02-8055323), which leaves several times a day from Piazza Castello. You can buy tickets on the tram; audio commentary in Italian, English, French and German. It is a 'hop-on hop-off' tour that takes from 1 hour 45 minutes to all day. Tickets are valid for the whole day.

Details on a combination bus/boat tour – the major sights by bus followed by a trip along the Naviglio Grande – can be obtained from the APT, Via Marconi 1.

Facts for the Visitor

VISAS
Visitors from the European Union (EU) require either a passport or identification card to enter Italy. Holders of passports from most other countries (including Australia, Canada, New Zealand and the United States) do not usually require a visa *(permesso di soggiorno)* for a period not exceeding 90 days.

CUSTOMS
If you are an EU visitor, there are no duty-free limits, provided that whatever you buy is for personal use. If you bring back more than the following guidance levels for consumer goods, customs may ask you to prove that the goods are for your own use: 800 cigarettes, 200 cigars, 1kg of tobacco, 90 litres of wine, 10 litres of spirit and 100 litres of beer per person. Travellers may bring an unlimited amount of Italian or foreign currency into Italy. However, on departure, any currency above the equivalent of €10,300 must be declared.

INFORMATION
Information can be obtained from the offices of the Italian State Tourist Office (ENIT) at the following:

Public holidays
1 January (New Year)
6 January (Epiphany, or Befana)
Easter Monday
25 April (Liberation Day)
1 May (Labour Day)
Ascension (date varies)
15 August (Assumption of the Virgin, or Ferragosto)
1 November (All Saints' Day)
7 December (Sant'Ambrogio, only in Milan)
8 December (the Immaculate Conception)
25–26 December (Christmas)

In the UK: Italian State Tourist Office, 1 Princes Street, London W1B 2AY, tel: 020-7408 1254; fax: 020-7493 6695; www.enit.it

In the US: Italian Government Tourist Office, 630 5th Avenue, Suite 1565, NY 10111, New York, tel: 212-245 4822; fax: 212-586 9249.

In Milan: Contact the provincial tourist information offices, the Azienda di Promozione Turistica (APT), which are open all year round. Addresses are as follows: Palazzo del Turismo, Via Marconi 1, tel: 02-72524301; fax: 02-72524350 (open Mon–Fri 8.45am–1pm, 2–6pm, Sat, Sun 9.30am–1pm, 2–5pm); Stazione Centrale, First Floor, tel: 02-7252 4360 (open Mon–Sat 9am–6.30pm, Sun 9.30am–12.30pm and 1.30–5pm). There are also tourist offices at Milan's two main airports.

Information sections listing the events of the coming week (theatre, cinema, concerts, etc) are included in the Wednesday edition of the Italian daily paper *Corriere della Sera* and the Thursday edition of *La Repubblica*. Also useful are *A Guest in Milan* or *Hello Milano*, available from major hotels, and *Milano Mese* (in English and Italian) from the tourist office.

Lakeside scene

MONEY, BANKS AND EXCHANGE

In common with most other European countries, the official currency used in Italy is the euro (€). Notes are denominated in 5, 10, 20, 50, 100 and 500 euros; coins are in 1 and 2 euros and 1, 2, 5, 10, 20 and 50 cents.

Banks are generally open Mon–Fri 8.30am–1.30pm and 2.30–4.30pm. The bank at Stazione Centrale is open every day from 8am–7pm. B*ureaux de change* are open every day until 7 or 8pm. Most credit cards, including Visa, Access and American Express, are accepted in hotels, restaurants and shops and for air and train tickets and cash at any bank. There are numerous cashpoints *(Bancomat)*, which commonly take Cirrus, Maestro, Mastercard and Visa.

Travellers Cheques (such as Thomas Cook and American Express) are widely accepted in Milan.

OPENING TIMES

Remember that many museums, churches and petrol stations close for lunch. Small shops (local stores, specialist shops, boutiques etc) are generally open from 9am–12.30pm and from 3.30–7.30pm, but large department stores, supermarkets and many of the shops in the city centre remain open all day.

Around 15 August, the time of *Ferragosto*, many shops, bars and museums are closed. Those open are listed in the daily papers or in the *Hello Milan* monthly guide.

Opening hours for the major museums are given in this guide (most are closed one day a week – usually Monday). For more details contact the APT.

POST
Milan's Posta Centrale (main post office) is at Via Cordusio 4. Stamps *(francobolli)* can be purchased from post offices and tobacconists *(tabacchi)*. Post boxes, which are red, usually have one slot for internal Milan post and another for everywhere else.

TELEPHONING
Nearly all phone boxes work with a phone card *(carta telefonica)*, which may be purchased at tobacconists or newsstands. Some phone boxes also take credit cards and coins.

To call abroad, dial 00 then the country code as follows: Australia 61; France 33; Germany 49; Japan 81; Spain 34; United Kingdom 44; US and Canada 1. If calling Milan (even a local call within the city) note that you must still dial the 02 code; if calling from abroad, the '0' from 02 is retained. For directory enquiries, dial 12.

TIME
Italy is one hour ahead of Greenwich Mean Time and six hours ahead of US Eastern Standard Time.

VOLTAGE
Usually 220v, occasionally 110v.

MEDICAL
With an E111 form from the Department of Health and Social Security, UK visitors are entitled to free medical treatment in Italy. However, it is

Bills and tipping
Restaurants are required by law to issue an official receipt to customers. VAT (IVA) will be included in the bill, but service *(servizio)* may be added as an extra, and in grander places there tends to be a cover charge *(coperto)* in addition to this. Even if you see the words *Servizio compreso*, a small tip is expected. Check the menu and bill carefully.

still very strongly advisable to take out travel insurance. Holiday insurance policies are highly recommended for non-EU visitors.

THEFT
Carry valuables close to your body and keep a firm hold on handbags. All cases of theft need to be reported immediately to the police *(Carabinieri)*; call their stolen-goods department *(Questura)* on 02-62261.

EMERGENCY NUMBERS
Ambulance: 118
Fire: 115
Police: 112
SOS Emergency Number: 113
Emergency Medical Aid: 02-3883

LOST AND FOUND
The city's **Ufficio oggetti rinvenuti**, Via Friuli 30 (tel: 02-5465299), is responsible for objects lost on trams, buses or metro trains (open Mon–Fri 8.30am–4pm, closed Sat and Sun). Another lost property office (Via Sammartini 108, tel: 02-67712677, open daily 7am–8pm) is responsible for objects lost on trains or in the station.

CONSULATES & EMBASSIES
British Consulate, Via San Paolo 7, tel: 02-723001.
US Consulate, via Principe Amedeo, tel: 02-290351 (for visas 02-290 35280).

ACCOMMODATION

There are two main points to note about accommodation in Milan: firstly, that it's all relatively expensive, with most of the hotels catering for the three-star market and above; secondly, that things tend to book up well in advance, especially during trade fairs or fashion weeks, so make sure you reserve.

Most of the city's hotels are set in the centre, especially around Piazza della Repubblica and Stazione Centrale, with others near La Fiera, the trade-fair centre. To book, contact your preferred hotel directly or call an agency such as Milano Hotels Central Booking, Piazza Missori (tel: 02-8054242/56; fax: 02-8054291). You can also visit: www.traveleurop.it

Milan's official hotel categories (one star to five star deluxe) can be misleading, with many of the less high-tech, inn-style hotels offering charm and an excellent service despite their low star rating. Always check whether breakfast and taxes are included in the price and if weekend/non-fair rates are available. During July and August you may be able to negotiate a lower rate if you deal directly with the hotel, as these months are low season.

Hotel Selection

The hotels below are divided into three categories: €€€ = expensive, €€ = moderate, € = inexpensive.

€€€

Cavour, Via Fatebenefratelli 21, tel: 02-6572051, fax: 02-6592263; www.hotelcavour.it Located in the fashion and designer district, the Quadrilatero, this modern hotel offers every comfort.
Executive Hotel, Via Don Luigi Sturzo 45, tel: 02-62942807, fax: 02-62942713; www.atahotels.it First-rate service, an elegant atmosphere and a good restaurant are all promised at this large hotel opposite Stazione Garibaldi.
Four Seasons, Via Gesù 8, tel: 02-77088, fax: 02-77085000; www.fourseasons.com/milan The Four Seasons is universally acknowledged as Milan's best hotel, both in terms of atmosphere and pure, unadulterated luxury. Converted from a 15th-century monastery, with lovely rooms overlooking delightful cloisters, it is favoured by celebrities and the fashion pack. It is also home to the magnificent Il Teatro gourmet restaurant (evenings only) and the less rarified La Terrazza restaurant.
Grand Hotel et de Milan, Via Manzoni 29, tel: 02-723141, fax: 02-8646 0861; www.grandhoteletdemilan.it Milan's most historic hotel, the Grand, was founded in 1863 and is sumptuously furnished with antiques. It is located on one of the city's most prestigious streets close to La Scala, and it was here that the composer Verdi died. It is home to the ever-popular Don Carlos restaurant.
Grand Hotel Duomo, Via San Raffaele, tel: 02-8833, fax: 02-86462027. Built in 1860 and recently redesigned, this hotel is in an excellent central location overlooking the Duomo – note that it is built in the same marble as that used for the cathedral. Some of the rooms and suites have film themes, and there's a lovely roof terrace.
Hermitage, Via Messina 10, tel: 02-33107700, fax: 02-33107399; www.monrifhotels.it This characterful, elegant hotel has 131 rooms (suites also available) and a delightful garden.
Hotel de la Ville, Via Hoepli 6, tel: 02-867651, fax: 02-866609. Gracious hotel in the heart of the fashion district. The rooms are understated and decorated with period furnishings. The

hotel is home to the Canova Restaurant and a discreet panelled bar, an elegant choice for tea or cocktails.

Meridien Excelsior Gallia, Piazza Duca d'Aosta 9, tel: 02-67851, fax: 02-66713239. Now renovated, this elegant yet welcoming place is one of the best hotels in Milan. Splendid breakfasts.

Principe di Savoia, Piazza della Repubblica 17, tel: 02-62301, fax: 02-6595838; www.luxurycollection.com Located north of the cathedral, this is a classic luxury hotel, offering superb service. It has elegant reception rooms, 399 bedrooms, a swimming pool, sauna and health/spa centre.

Sheraton Diana Majestic, Viale Piave 42, tel: 02-29513404, fax: 02-201072; www.sheraton.com/dianamajestic.com Situated near Porta Venezia is this well-renovated art nouveau/art deco hotel, converted from Milan's first public swimming baths (1842). It has Empire-style bedrooms and attractive public rooms and is popular with models and fashion designers.

€€

Antica Locanda Leonardo, Corso Magenta 78, tel: 02-463317, fax: 02-48019012; www.lelloc.com This small, family-run hotel offers a warm welcome and enjoys an enviable location close to Santa Maria delle Grazie.

Useful websites
www.ambitalia.org.uk (Italian Embassy/Consulate site)
www.ciaomilano.com (Milan tourist board site)
www.enit.it (Italian Tourist Board web page)
www.hellomilano.it (city magazine online)
www.inlombardia.it (Lombardy site)
www.meteo.it (the weather in Italy online)
www.milanocastello.it (Castello Sforzesco)
www.museionline.it (Italian museum site)
www.teatro.it (Italian theatre site)
www.ticket.it (ticket reservation in Italy online)
www.trenitalia.it (Italian railways online)

Antica Locanda dei Mercanti, Via San Tomaso 6, tel: 02-8054080, fax: 02-8054090; www.locanda.it A small, but gorgeous hotel set in an 18th-century palace near La Scala. Each room is individually decorated, but common features include personal 'libraries', wrought-iron bedsteads, unusual rugs, fresh flowers and marble bathrooms. A real gem.

Antica Locanda Solferino, Via Castelfidardo 2, tel: 02-6570129, fax: 02-6571361; www.anticalocandasolferino.it In a great location in the lively Brera district is the Antica Locanda Solferino, another lovely old-fashioned, thoroughly

Milan is ideal for a romantic weekend

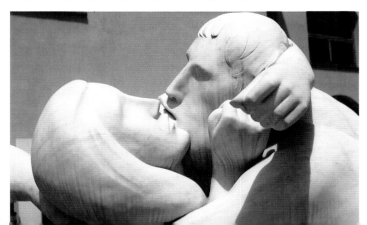

romantic hotel. The rooms are furnished with antiques, and most have very good-sized bathrooms; breakfast is served on beautifully presented trays in your room. The owners are friendly and speak good English. The hotel is very popular, so book well in advance. The fabulous Ristorante Solferino *(see page 115)* is just next door.

Ariston, Largo Carrobbio 2, tel: 02-72000556, fax: 02-72000914; www.brerahotels.com/ariston The Ariston is a so-called 'ecological' hotel, managing to be both environmentally correct and comfortable. Rooms are well furnished, and the atmosphere is friendly. All guests have unlimited use of the hotel bicycles. Handy for the canal district.

Century Tower, Via Fabio Filzi, tel: 02-67504, fax: 02-66980602. This hotel offers spacious suites, a welcoming atmosphere and a good-value restaurant. Weekend rates available.

Manzoni, Via Santo Spirito 20, tel: 02-76005700. fax: 02-784212; www.hotel manzoni.com Built during the 1950s in the heart of the upmarket fashion district, the medium-sized (49 rooms) Manzoni offers good value for money and an excellent location. Caring family service combines with pleasant decoration

and good facilities (room service, bar and a garage) to ensure a pleasant stay.

Palazzo delle Stelline, Corso Magenta 61, tel: 02-4818431; www.hotelpalazzo dellestelline.it A lovely, atmospheric hotel with its own restaurant, all set in a former orphanage in one of the city's most upmarket districts.

Radisson sas Bonaparte, Via Cusani, tel: 02-85601, fax: 02- 8693601. A small, discreet and chic hotel in a central location by the Castello Sforzesco. Good service.

Radisson sas Scandinavia, Via Fauché 15, tel: 02-336391, fax: 02-33104510. This elegant hotel has a relaxed atmosphere and is very convenient for trade-fair centre.

€

Adriatico, Via Conca dei Navigli 20, tel: 02-58104141, fax: 02 89401012. Pleasant, aptly named hotel in the lively canal quarter.

Aspromonte, Piazza Aspromonte 12/14, tel: 02-2361119, fax: 02-2367621; www.venere.it/milano/aspromonte The Aspromonte is a small, gracious place, where attentive service is given by the young proprietors. In summer breakfast is served in the garden.

Cristoforo Colombo, Corso Buenos Aires 3, tel: 02-29406214, fax: 02-29516096. Set in the bustling shopping district of Buenos Aires, the Cristoforo Colombo is handy for the trade-fair centre. The rooms vary considerably in size and quality, so request a large, light one at the front.

Europeo, Via Canonica 38, tel: 02-3314751, fax: 02-33105410. Set near the trade fair centre, this is one of the few Milan hotels with a garden and outdoor pool.

Gran Duca di York, Via Moneta 1a, tel: 02-874863, fax: 02-8690344. Lovely hotel housed in an old *palazzo* near the Pinacoteca di Brera. Closed in August.

> ### Youth hostels and camping
> If your budget doesn't quite stretch to inflated Milanese hotel prices, there are alternatives. Milan's Ostella Rotta youth hostel is at Viale Salmoiraghi 2, tel: 02-39267095 (metro M1 in the direction of Molino Dorino as far as Piazzale Lotto, or bus 91 from Stazione Centrale). The hostel is open 7–9am (breakfast/departure) and 5pm–12.30am. Milan's campsites are all located outside the city, at: Autodromo di Monza, north of the Parco di Monza, tel: 039-387771; fax: 039-320324 (open Apr–Sept) or Città di Milano, Via G. Airaghi 61, tel: 02 4820 0134; fax: 02 48202999 (open all year round).

❊ INSIGHT COMPACT GUIDES

Great Little Guides to the following destinations:

Algarve	Finland	Rhodes	Jersey
Amsterdam	Florence	Rio de Janeiro	Lake District
Antigua/Barbuda	French Riviera	Rome	London
Athens	Goa	St. Lucia	New Forest
Bahamas	Gran Canaria	St. Petersburg	North York Moors
Bali	Greece	Salzburg	Northumbria
Bangkok	Holland	Shanghai	Oxford
Barbados	Hong Kong	Singapore	Peak District
Barcelona	Ibiza	Southern Spain	Scotland
Beijing	Iceland	Sri Lanka	Scottish
Belgium	Ireland	Switzerland	Highlands
Berlin	Israel	Sydney	Shakespeare
Bermuda	Italian Lakes	Tahiti	Country
Brittany	Italian Riviera	Tenerife	Snowdonia
Bruges	Jamaica	Thailand	South Downs
Brussels	Jerusalem	Toronto	York
Budapest	Kenya	Turkey	Yorkshire Dales
Burgundy	Laos	Turkish Coast	
California	Lisbon	Tuscany	USA regional:
Cambodia	Madeira	Venice	Boston
Cancún & the	Madrid	Vienna	Cape Cod
Yucatán	Mallorca	Vietnam	Chicago
Chile	Malta	West of Ireland	Florida
Copenhagen	Menorca		Florida Keys
Costa Brava	Milan	UK regional:	Hawaii – Maui
Costa del Sol	Montreal	Bath &	Hawaii – Oahu
Costa Rica	Morocco	Surroundings	Las Vegas
Crete	Moscow	Belfast	Los Angeles
Cuba	Munich	Cambridge &	Martha's Vineyard
Cyprus	Normandy	East Anglia	& Nantucket
Czech Republic	Norway	Cornwall	Miami
Denmark	Paris	Cotswolds	New Orleans
Dominican	Poland	Devon & Exmoor	New York
Republic	Portugal	Edinburgh	San Diego
Dublin	Prague	Glasgow	San Francisco
Egypt	Provence	Guernsey	Washington DC

Insight's checklist to meet all your travel needs:

- ■ *Insight Guides* provide the complete picture, with expert cultural background and stunning photography. Great for travel planning, for use on the spot, and as a souvenir. 186 titles.
- ■ *Insight Museums & Galleries* guides to London, Paris, Florence and New York provide comprehensive coverage of each city's cultural temples and lesser known collections.
- ■ *Insight Pocket Guides* focus on the best choices for places to see and things to do, picked by our correspondents. They include large fold-out maps. More than 130 titles.
- ■ *Insight Compact Guides* are the fact-packed books to carry with you for easy reference when you're on the move in a destination. More than 130 titles.
- ■ *Insight FlexiMaps* combine clear, detailed cartography with essential information and a laminated finish that makes the maps durable and easy to fold. 133 titles.

The world's largest collection of visual travel guides and maps

INDEX